VITAL SIGNS

A GUIDE TO HEALTHY LEADERSHIP
FOR PHYSICIANS

WHAT PEOPLE ARE SAYING

With precision and compassion, Dr. James Ice equips physician leaders to assess the true health of their leadership and organizations—not just by what's visible on the surface, but by recognizing deeper patterns, early warning signs, and pathways to long-term resilience. This is far more than a framework—it's a lifeline for those navigating complexity, burnout, and the demands of modern medicine. His approach equips physicians to lead with the insight needed to build cultures that thrive.

> —**Dr. Marshall Goldsmith,** Thinkers50 #1 Executive Coach and New York Times bestselling author of *The Earned Life, Triggers,* and *What Got You Here Won't Get You There.*

Dr. Jim Ice has assembled an insightful and creative perspective on leadership, organizational structure, and facilitating positive change. I have experienced Jim's expertise and insight firsthand, and I know others will benefit from the value of this new book.

> —**Robert L. Ferris**, MD, PhD, Lineberger Distinguished Professor and Executive Director, Lineberger Comprehensive Cancer Center, University of North Carolina

In today's complex healthcare landscape, physician-leaders face unprecedented internal and external pressures that demand exceptional leadership skills to successfully deliver on their organization's mission. Dr. Ice's 'Vital Signs' is an invaluable resource that provides practical, evidence-based guidance for navigating these challenges with wisdom and effectiveness.

This is far more than a theoretical text—it's a practical toolkit that belongs on every physician-leader's desk as an essential reference guide.

> —**Hy Simhan**, MD, MS, Professor, Vice Chair, OBGYN, University of Pittsburgh

This book is a lifeline for physicians leaders. The HEART Protocol is an insightful evidence-based framework that reminds us that great leadership begins within, empowering physicians to lead with courage, clarity, and compassion.

—**Amer Kaissi**, Ph.D., author of *Humbitious: The Power of Low-Ego, High-Drive Leadership*

Since the art of leadership is rarely taught in med school, executive coach Jim Ice has come to the rescue with a prescription for healthcare leadership. The HEART healthy leadership framework at the center of his book, Vital Signs, is a memorable and actionable roadmap for physicians leading others who care for others.

—**Scott Eblin**, two-time bestselling author and host of the Best Ever Podcast

In the crowded field of leadership literature, Vital Signs for Organizations is a true standout read. By translating organizational health into a language that is both practical and deeply human, Jim Ice captures the essence of what is needed to help organizations not just perform but thrive. With the clever and memorable HEART Protocol, Ice offers leaders a diagnostic tool as intuitive as it is powerful—grounded in research, rich with real-world application, and written with Ice's characteristic clarity with humility.

His approach is not just about improving performance; it's about cultivating cultures where people thrive. As Ice reminds us, 'Just as a healthy heart is central to human life, a healthy HEART is essential for an organization's longevity and success.' Whether you're leading a clinical team or a corporate one, this book will sharpen your thinking and help you build healthy, vibrant teams.

—**Ann Bowers-Evangelista**, Psy.D., MBA, Leadership Psychologist, Executive Coach, and Author of *The Endurance Leader*

If you're a physician leader seeking clarity, confidence, and practical tools to elevate your impact, I highly recommend reading Jim Ice's two-part Vital Sign series. These companion books are more than leadership guides—they're diagnostic and treatment manuals for the HEART of leadership and organizational health. Each book offers actionable insights, real-world examples, and tools to help leaders and organizations assess their "vital signs" and take preventive or corrective action.

His books reflect the same thoughtful, grounded, and empowering approach he brings to his coaching. Whether you're just stepping into leadership or looking to reinvigorate your team or organization, these books—and Jim—are invaluable resources.

—**Liron Pantanowitz**, MD, PhD, MHA, Professor, Chair Department Pathology, University of Pittsburgh

This powerful Vital Signs two-book framework—offers a mirrored approach to leadership and organizational health. Together, they form a comprehensive guide for diagnosing, treating, and preventing the behaviors and dynamics that impact performance, culture, and resilience.

At the core of each book is the concept of vital signs—key indicators that, like a medical check-up, help assess the health of a leader or organization. These signs offer a practical protocol grounded not only in research but also in lived experience and the diverse languages of leadership.

The HEART Series is rich with real-world stories and examples drawn from the author's personal and professional experience as well as interviews with physician leaders, educators, and executives. These voices bring the framework to life, offering insight into the challenges and triumphs of leadership in complex environments.

—**Martina Bison-Huckaby**, MBA, ACC, SHRM-SCP, Manager, Physician Learning and Development

In today's rapidly evolving healthcare landscape, physician leaders are called to lead not only with clinical expertise but with strategic clarity and human-centered purpose. Leadership development is a critical investment in their ability to inspire teams, foster trust, and drive meaningful change. As demands on healthcare systems intensify and the industry becomes more complex, equipping physician leaders with the tools to lead with resilience, emotional intelligence, and vision is essential. It's how we support not only the well-being and efficacy of our physician leaders, but also the vitality of the organizations, patients, and communities they serve.

—**Tony Gigliotti**, Talent Management Leader (Healthcare)

Jim Ice delivers a rare blend of heart, wisdom, and actionable insight in Vital Signs, a two-book series that redefines what it means to lead in healthcare. Designed for physician leaders, this powerful resource introduces the HEART Protocol, a clear, practical framework for strengthening both personal and organizational leadership health. Through compelling stories, real-world tools, and decades of experience, Jim offers more than guidance, he equips physicians to lead with authenticity, clarity, and impact. Vital Signs doesn't just inform, it transforms. This is essential reading for any physician ready to move beyond clinical excellence and into truly effective leadership.

—**Joel Garfinkle**, Executive Coach to Senior Leaders in Life Sciences
and author of *Executive Presence: Step Into Your Power, Convey
Confidence, & Lead with Conviction*

Effective and efficient physician leadership is essential to ultimate success of complex and matrixed healthcare organizations. Generally, physicians are trained towards achieving clinical, teaching and research excellence. They possess firsthand insight into clinical challenges, making them uniquely positioned to drive meaningful change. Equipping physicians with leadership skills enhances their ability to influence organizational strategy, improve interdisciplinary collaboration, and implement evidence-based practices effectively. Dr. Ice has been a trusted partner to me in my strategic efforts to best prepare physician leaders.

—**Mike Anderson**, VP HR – Physician Services

The Vital Signs HEART Protocol is exactly what today's leaders need. James provides some real practical insights that many physician and startup leaders especially need, as they typically grow into leadership roles through deep expertise rather than formal training. The book's medical metaphor makes the content very relatable and actionable, offering a clear framework for diagnosing and treating real leadership and organizational challenges. Having worked directly with James on coaching and leadership development initiatives, I've seen firsthand how his methods inspire accountability, resilience, and meaningful culture change. While many leadership books just give theory, Vital Signs is a real playbook that works in the real world."

—**Brad Ryba**, Tech Executive & 10X Performance Coach

vital signs

A GUIDE TO

HEALTHY LEADERSHIP

FOR PHYSICIANS

JAMES ICE, Ed.D. BCC

ISBN 978-1-960378-33-0   (paperback)
ISBN 978-1-960378-34-7   (ePub)

1ˢᵗ Edition

Book design by Anna Hall

ACKNOWLEDGEMENTS

I am deeply grateful to the physician leaders I have had the privilege to work alongside. Your honesty, determination, and commitment, both to patients and your organizations, have been the inspiration for these books. The *HEART leadership protocol* is drawn directly from the challenges you face, the insights you've shared, and the examples you've set.

To the team at Ascender Book Services (www.ascenderbook.services)—Kyle, Stephen, and Anna—thank you for your guidance, partnership, and flexibility. Together, we have brought my vision for these books to life, and I am grateful for the care and creativity you invested throughout the publishing process.

This work reflects the ongoing journey of physician leadership—one that requires courage, accountability, and vision. To those who pick up this book, I extend the same challenge I have seen my clients embrace: to put these principles into practice. Use them to strengthen your teams, to build healthier organizations, and to lead with the same dedication you bring to the care of your patients.

Contents

When stepping into leadership, recognize that clinical excellence alone isn't enough. Leading an organization requires the ability to apply analytical thinking and recognize the influencing systems while taking a larger strategic perspective. You must shift how you think.

Proactively consider how you want to show up in the leadership role. What's your leadership brand? What are the guiding principles you want to demonstrate through your leadership actions? These are foundational elements each leader should consider.

Learn how to cascade key messages, practice delivering feedback with emotional sensitivity, and demonstrate active listening. One of the best investments you can make is developing your communication and emotional intelligence skills. Take time to develop new skills in influence as a change agent, especially if you're leading peers. Whether it's restructuring, improving patient access, or adopting new technology, success hinges on how well you learn to lead the transition.

Finally, remember your own health and balance matter too. Set boundaries, delegate when needed, and make time for personal reflection and renewal. That's not selfish. That's sustainable leadership. Invest in your professional and support networks. The more perspectives you are exposed to, the more adaptive and insightful your leadership becomes. The best investment you can make for your team is to invest in your development as their leader.

—Summary of interviews with physician leader educators on their
recommendations for physicians moving into leadership roles

Introduction:
The HEART Protocol

When I was a lad of five, the sights, sounds, and unique smells of the Buckwheat Festival in rural West Virginia captivated my young imagination. By the time evening fell, those fairgrounds in my birthplace of Kingwood were packed with families, everyone sharing in the excitement of the Ferris wheel and the spinning rides and the challenges of the carneys' games. But as my parents and I stood in a long, winding line along the perimeter of the fairgrounds, I only had one thing on my mind: buckwheat cakes. The line led to the assembly hall, the local fire station, where the firefighters had volunteered to serve pancakes made from the festival's namesake buckwheat flour. For a small donation, you could order as many of the tangy cakes as you could eat, each one smothered with maple syrup and garnished with sausage—lots of sausage.

These pancakes were a once-per-year treat for my family, so the only thing that could dampen my anticipation was the sight of the line itself, which looked endless to my young eyes. My parents, meanwhile, seemed to know everyone, so they passed the time talking to those in line or wandering by on their way to view the livestock or taste the homemade pies on offer at a nearby stand. Lost in my imagination, I found myself distracted by the flashing lights unique to the festival.

Then it happened. A rather large man who had been standing in line four or five people ahead of us let out a loud groan and tumbled headfirst down the embankment into the fairgrounds. From my limited vantage point, I could see that he had been badly injured from the fall and was bleeding from a gash to his forehead, his arm bent at an unnatural angle. He lay still, eyes closed, no longer moaning. Horror and fear showed on the faces of those standing with us in line. I was scared too.

That was when my father did something that frightened me even more: He slid down the hill, sidled up next to the unconscious man, and started beating him squarely on the chest. Another man soon joined my father and began doing something near the unconscious man's head, but I couldn't quite make it out. All I could see was my father delivering one violent blow after another. As he straddled the man's ample belly, Dad looked like he was trying to knock the breath out of him with each blow. My mother knelt beside me to put her comforting arms around me. I turned to her in fear and confusion and pressed my face to her shoulder, hiding my eyes.

These were the days before cell phones, of course, but word of the incident quickly spread up and down the long line. Minutes later, several firefighters raced over to the injured man, his body still limp, and took over for my father and his companion. Soon the man was on a cart, then in the back of an ambulance, and then on his way to the local hospital. One of the firemen approached my father. My anxiety grew, for I was sure Dad was about to be punished for his mistreatment of the man. Instead, the fireman shook my father's hand and patted him on the back.

Soon, buckwheat cakes started coming off the griddle again, and the line reassembled. When Dad returned to our place in line, others also shook his hand and even thanked him for his quick response.

By the time we finally sat down to eat, I was full of questions. "Why were you beating that man?" I asked. "Why's everybody congratulating you?"

"That man had a heart attack," answered my father, who was a certified first-aid instructor at the local power generation station where he worked. "During a heart attack, when the heart stops beating, it must be started again as quickly as possible."

My father's actions, which I had perceived as violent, had been designed to restore life, not take it away.

Once I understood that he had been trying to rescue the man, more questions flooded my mind. "I saw him bleeding," I said. "And his arm looked broken. Why didn't you take care of that stuff first?"

"When delivering first aid," he explained, "injuries are treated according to priority. At the top of the list is resuscitating the victim's heart and his breathing. Then other injuries can be addressed. By striking the man's chest, I was trying to restart his heart. The man helping me was breathing for him by blowing air into his mouth until he could breathe on his own. Together, we were trying to keep his blood flowing—to keep him alive—until his heart and lungs could function on their own again." To effectively triage a first-aid case, medical providers follow a protocol for treatment.

I'd love to offer you a happy ending and say that the injured man recovered and lived to a ripe old age, thanks to my father's actions. Unfortunately, I never learned of his fate. To me, he would forever remain an unknown man in a river of people waiting in a long line. I don't know his medical history, his daily habits, or (aside from buckwheat cakes) his taste for rich foods. But I *do* know that once his heart had stopped beating, unless restarted, he would have died. The heart, often taken for granted, must be the initial priority. It enables the operations of the numerous systems within the human body, and when it fails, life is over.

We recognize the central role of heart health in any medical procedure. Even during the annual checkup, after we engage in the obligatory lying about our weight, the medical professional first diagnoses our heart health. Additionally, prior to any significant medical procedure, our heart health is assessed. If our heart is strong, the procedure continues. If, however, there are concerns about our heart health, the procedure is often postponed until heart health has improved. Why? Because heart health is critical to not only the proper functioning of every part of our body but also the effective recovery. Hearth health is what I call *priority protocol*.

PRIORITY PROTOCOL

Based on that opening story, you might think this book is about living a "heart-healthy" lifestyle. And in a way, you'd be right, though it's important to note that I'm not a cardiologist or a nutritionist. I am an organizational sociologist. For more than three decades, I've worked with and studied hundreds of organizations and their leaders. I've discovered what I believe to be a priority protocol for the health of an organization and its leaders.

Just as we desire to ensure our physical health, leaders are concerned about the health of their teams. They want to know how to assess and treat the critical systems within their organization. The symptoms of an ailing organization are often quite apparent (e.g., poor performance metrics, high turnover, etc.), but is there an organized way to diagnose and treat an ailing organization? In medicine, a treatment protocol can guide the health-care professional in their health assessment and development of a related treatment plan. This protocol defines the methodology for assessment and data collection and suggests the treatments and interventions to be performed, their potential impact (both positive and adverse), and how to measure progress toward health. If only there was a leadership protocol that could help us as leaders look beyond the presenting symptoms to understand what factors are impacting the overall health of the organization.

Organizations are complex organisms, just like the human body. They are living, adaptive systems made up of interdependent subsystems that must work together to survive and thrive in a changing environment. Like the human body, organizations interact with and respond to their external environment, adjusting their structure and processes to maintain health and effectiveness. As an organizational consultant, I'm often asked by leaders to help them understand how to know if their organizations are healthy and growing as they desire. My response often surprises them when I ask, "How is your HEART health?"

Just as heart health is central to the health of our bodies, an organization's HEART is central to organizational health. The organizational HEART provides the lifeblood (energy source) that flows to feed and support every system, function, and action taken by the organization. Just as human heart health is the starting point of any medical health diagnosis, the organization HEART health is the priority protocol for the assessment and treatment of overall organizational health.

> If only there was a leadership protocol that could help us as leaders look beyond the presenting symptoms to understand what factors are impacting the overall health of the organization.

Allow me to illustrate this organizational HEART assessment in practice. Whenever I enter an organization, the priority protocol guides me to start asking questions and making observations about behaviors that fall into five areas.

The first is about the overall health of the organization's strategy and culture. Is there a *healthy strategy* that focuses resources and attention toward organizational mission and priorities? I look closely at the vision and mission of the organization to determine how well these key grounding elements are articulated. Do the strategies take into consideration the current and future environment? Are the action plans and operating priorities aligned to this strategy? Do the team members understand and buy into these strategies? I look to understand if the *culture is healthy*. Is it a culture that supports engagement, holds people accountable, and fosters supportive and high-performing teams? Or is it a culture that's focused on the outcomes of individuals rather than the whole? Do the team members see the culture as growth-oriented or toxic?

Next, I diagnosis the following: How *engaged* are the people in the organization in the strategic mission and vision? Do they understand it? Are they motivated by it? Are they committed to it? Is the organizational culture integrated with that mission and vision? Is that connection driving desired outcomes within the organization?

The third thing I look for is how *accountable* the people are within the organization, both the leaders and the employees. Specifically, what I mean here is this: Are they accountable not just for activity but for results? Maybe you've been in an organization where people aren't properly connected to the vision or mission. In such organizations, you can feel the lack of energy. Or perhaps you've been in an organization where people don't take personal accountability for outcomes, and no one owns failure. In such an organization, when people don't hold each other accountable for outcomes, both good and bad, results suffer, and over time the organization fails.

The fourth area I assess is based on a lesson that COVID-19 taught us well: that we need to be prepared to bounce back—or bounce *forward*, as I prefer to say—from difficult situations. COVID-19 put us in a situation where organizations have had to demonstrate their resilience, first to adapt to a new kind of working environment and then to adapt to produce at pre-COVID levels. With or without a pandemic, if you consider the amount of change that organizations go through, how often they see disruptions to the status quo, it's critical to develop grit in organizations and their leaders. Can they change and be agile in response to pressures within their industry, from their competition, and within their competitive needs and advantages? Are they *resilient*?

Finally, my priority protocol has me studying an organization's ability to coordinate and cooperate. How well do leaders and employees work as a ***team***? How do their teams function together across organizational and functional boundaries? Are they maximizing the capability of the company by leveraging each other as well as they could? Is there a team-based culture here? Again, you've probably been in organizations where the teams demonstrate great camaraderie, where there's this high level of trust and performance, where they can hold each other accountable, where they can have difficult conversations with each other. But I'm sure you've also been on the other side of that, where people tend to engage in finger-pointing, refuse to take accountability, and are quick to come up with excuses and throw other team members under the bus.

You might have noticed that these five areas fit neatly into a memorable acronym. Is an organization Healthy? Engaged? Accountable? Resilient? And does it demonstrate Team behaviors? These behaviors form the HEART of an organization:

- Healthy: ensuring the well-being of enabling systems.
- Engaged: investing in mission and vision.
- Accountable: owning actions and outcomes.
- Resilient: bouncing forward from setbacks.
- Team-oriented: collaborating toward mutual goals.

Consider your experience with the many organizations with which you interact professionally, socially, and even as a customer. Can you see how each HEART component affects an organization's effectiveness, ability to achieve its mission, and its reputation in the marketplace? Perhaps you've had experience with toxic work cultures or have seen the impact of employees that refuse to take accountability to ensure excellence in execution or customer service. I hope you've had the experience of working on a team whose members were engaged, accountable to personal and team outcomes, and found ways to support and enable each other, even in times of significant change.

By researching both successful and unsuccessful teams, I came to the realization that each organization has a HEART, and the health of that HEART is critical to the successful operation of every system, process, and transaction. Those organizations that excel share the characteristics described, and those that struggle typically lack one or more. Sure, there are thousands of systems and ongoing functions across any organization, but just like the human heart is priority one of health-care providers, these HEART behaviors are priority protocol for leaders seeking long-term organizational health. This book will help you learn about the *vital signs* of HEART health or disease and recommend targeted treatment actions for HEART health.

Just as my father did while trying to save the man at the Buckwheat Festival, when assessing organizations, we need to check on the **HEART of the organization** first—the factors that drive not only cultural outcomes but performance outcomes and financial outcomes as well. An organization might be in serious financial trouble, for example, or morale among the employees might be at an all-time low, but like the laceration or broken arm of the man in my story, such problems can't be effectively addressed until we've stabilized the HEART of the organization. A failing HEART is an emergency that requires immediate intervention. The HEART Protocol is a powerful tool in diagnosing and treating the organizational HEART.

HEART OF A LEADER

For some years now, I've been using this framework to help my clients understand how to diagnose and treat the **HEART of their organization**. Recently, during a series of executive coaching meetings, I found myself encouraging my executive clients to think about their own HEART health in terms of how they organize and live as a leader. How engaged are they in leadership? How are they accountable as a leader? Are they resilient as a leader? And do they have the team built around them to support their goals as a leader?

It soon became clear that there are two equally important, symbiotic components of this priority protocol—two sections of the HEART, like the atria and ventricles if you will. So this two-part series will address both how to diagnose and treat the **HEART of the organization** and the **HEART of the leader**.

The book you are holding is one of two books that fit together as a unit. The first is aimed at helping the organizational leader better understand how to diagnose, treat, and prevent motivations and behaviors that could be keeping them from functioning at full HEART capacity as a leader. The second, meanwhile, is geared toward the organization itself. Each has been written to complement the other while standing on its own. Each provides insights as well as practical methods and tools to develop a healthy HEART.

Too often, when confronted with organizational health issues—whether emanating from outside the organization (e.g., changing markets, falling revenue) or from within (e.g., lagging employee morale, ethical or moral violations)—leaders address only the symptoms and thus miss the more urgent underlying health issue. This book will teach you how to see the HEART the same way a physician sees the human heart: as a tireless workhorse that powers everything around it and without which nothing can function.

In health and in crisis, the physician monitors a patient's heart health first. This allows them to establish a heart health baseline for the patient before they design the best treatment plan for their patient's ailments. This resource is designed to facilitate your ability as a leader to diagnose the HEART health. This allows you to establish the HEART health baseline and to better define the preventive or corrective actions required to ensure the health of the organization and its leader. A healthy HEART is required to ensure the safe, effective, and lasting intervention into other presenting ailments. It is a priority protocol. This book presents a proven pathway for treating the HEART: the HEART Protocol. You have, no doubt, noticed by now that when referring to the behaviors of a Healthy, Engaged, Accountable, Resilient, and Team-Oriented leader or organization, we will use capital letters for HEART to distinguish from the physical heart.

HOW TO USE THIS RESOURCE

Keeping with the heart health metaphor, I found it useful to organize this resource to help the reader *diagnose* and *treat* the health of the HEART. This book, as well as its companion, *Vital Signs: A Guide to Healthy Organizations for Physicians*, and the dozens of related resources accessible on the ***Vitalsigns-book.com*** website, are designed to assist you in developing your "leadership practice." They're not textbooks, presenting the latest and greatest theories, although you'll see the application of theories in practice throughout. Nor are they parables of another's leadership journey, although you'll hear stories of leadership successes and failures. They *are* designed to be practical guides to assist you along your leadership journey. You may choose to read each resource guide from beginning to end, or you can pick and choose to read a specific chapter or vital sign description based on the challenges you're facing currently. As an introduction to or a refresher on proven leadership practices, the *Vital Signs* books are designed to inform you, challenge you, equip you, and encourage you to be the leader you aspire to be. My simple objective for these books is that they make it to the shelf by your desk, where you can keep and use them as important reference guides.

This first book is designed for you to focus first on your HEART health as a leader. Effective leaders recognize that their personal HEART health has a direct impact on the HEART health of their organization. They invest in their own development as a leader, recognizing the multiplicative impact this investment can have across the many team members. They're willing to do the difficult work that Michael Jackson recommended of "starting with the man [or woman] in the mirror" before trying to diagnose the health of the organization or organizations they lead. This is hard work, and I appreciate your interest in taking this personal step to carefully assess your own health. "Do as I say, not as I do" is the easier alternative. Unfortunately, there are many examples of physicians who do not live by the heart-healthy recommendations they suggest for their patients. It's hard to hear and take seriously the health recommendation that we should drop a few pounds for better heart health from a physician who's significantly overweight. It's even more difficult to hear how we should change our behavior to improve our HEART-healthy behaviors from a leader who doesn't demonstrate them.

I've heard it said that "doctors make the worst patients." Taking a close look at ourselves isn't easy. It's so much easier to see HEART-unhealthy behaviors in others. It requires honest self-reflection and commitment to address unhealthy HEART behaviors in ourselves as leaders. However, just like an investment in exercise, proper diet, and adequate sleep contribute to a healthy lifestyle and longer life, your HEART-healthy behaviors as a leader will improve the impact and enjoyment of your leadership tenure. I chose to start each chapter with a list of the *presenting symptoms* of lack of HEART health. These describe the indicators of potential diseases related to each element of the HEART. Take a look at each list to see how HEART disease presents itself when each component of the HEART is not functioning as it should.

Each chapter briefly explains the importance of one of the HEART components. For each HEART component, we review four *vital signs* that will help you assess, monitor, and treat HEART health. The discussion of research and practical applications around each vital sign will enable you to define a health baseline, establish early detection systems for potential health problems, and create a *treatment plan* to address the presenting and anticipated health needs.

At the end of each chapter, there are two specific recommendations for *preventive action* you can take to support the healthy development of each topic. Just as a heart-healthy diet and proper exercise can strengthen and protect the human heart, these recommendations can help you strengthen and protect the HEART behaviors. There are also *tools* available on my website, *vitalsigns-book.com/resources*, designed to assist you in diagnosing and treating HEART health. Consider these resources your HEART health first-aid kit.

· · ·

John Maxwell, renowned leadership guru, reminds us, "You cannot lead others until you first lead yourself. You can lead yourself at your best only if you invest in yourself first."[1] Additionally he suggests, "The moment you stop learning is the moment you stop leading." A commitment to continuous learning is the investment an effective leader makes for themselves and for their team.

These books are dedicated to helping leaders understand the unique function of the HEART of the leader and the HEART of the organization. After reading them, you'll understand how to monitor HEART health, ensure its proper nourishment and exercise, and avoid the consequences of HEART disease. The HEART's function is not a matter of casual concern but a priority protocol for organizational health and your health as its leader.

H-ealthy
E-ngaged
A-ccountable
R-esilient
T-eam

The HEART Protocol

If leadership drains you instead of energizing you, something needs to change. As Atul Gawande put it, "I get nurtured by what I do. It feeds me." If you're constantly exhausted and unfulfilled, it's a sign. Either the role isn't right, or you need to adjust how you engage with it.

And just like you wouldn't tell a patient to quit smoking while lighting up a cigarette yourself, you can't lead effectively without taking care of your own health. Sleep, nutrition, and mental well-being aren't optional. They're essential to bringing your best self to the role.

Leadership isn't a solo act. Having a coach, therapist, or mentor outside your chain of command gives you space to focus on yourself. They provide an objective perspective on you and what you can bring to making the connections required of an effective leader.

—Summary of interview with a physician leader: Chief, Internal Medicine

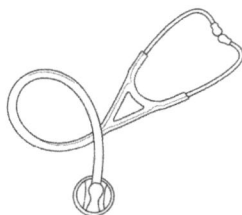

The H-ealthy Leader

"Who we are is how we lead."
—Brené Brown[2]

PRESENTING SYMPTOMS ADDRESSED IN THIS CHAPTER

Lacking motivation for work.	Burning out others.
Pulled in too many directions.	Negative thinking.
Lack of trust from your staff.	Lack of work-life balance.
Signs of addiction potential.	Lack of time for self.

When we think about leadership, we must first think about who we are, because our beliefs, character traits, and behaviors directly reflect how we lead. If we understand the former, we can properly evaluate the latter.

But before we can delve into who we are, let's take a step back and think about what it means to lead a group. Do you remember the old game show *Name That Tune*? Contestants competed against each other to see who could name a tune in the shortest number of notes. I often play a facsimile of that game with my clients when I'm teaching the subject of leadership. I ask them, "Can you define leadership in three words?" Typically, they answer with words like *integrity*, *transparency*, *respect*, and so on.

Hundreds—maybe thousands—of books have been written on leadership, and each book offers a different definition of its principal subject. One of the best is Peter Northouse's *Leadership*, which I often use when teaching undergrads and graduate students. Northouse defines it as follows: "Leadership is a process by which an individual influences a group of individuals to achieve a common goal."[3] But the only definition that's important at this point is *your* definition. What do *you* mean when you say leadership? What will be your three words?

I begin my definition of leadership with one word, and that word is *influence*. Like Northouse, I believe that leadership, at its core, is influence. A true leader, regardless of the position they hold, wields an outsized influence over the people around them.

> Leadership is a process by which an individual influences a group of individuals to achieve a common goal.

We've all worked for someone who wasn't a very good leader. They didn't really influence our behaviors because we didn't have respect for them. But the ability to influence someone else, because it forms the bedrock of true leadership, doesn't require an official position of leadership. In fact, some of the most influential people I've worked with over the years have been my peers, and sometimes they were the employees themselves who worked for me, because they had the greatest influence on the decisions we made and the actions we took. They were leaders because they influenced others to follow them. Such a power—the ability to inspire others to follow you—can be used for good or evil. Consider Jesus Christ and Martin Luther King Jr. on the one hand and Joseph Stalin and Adolph Hitler on the other.

Again, true leadership, the ability to inspire others to follow you, is not specific to a position—or even a personality type or level of education. It can come from someone above, below, or beside you in the organizational hierarchy. All that matters is the leader's ability to influence. The better someone is able to influence those around them, the stronger they are as a leader.

Understood in this context, influence is a verb. It's something a leader *does*. Leadership, then, isn't a label or a position conferred upon us. It's an ability we exercise. And it's often situation-specific. If you're a surgeon, for example, you might be a highly competent leader in the operating room but a less proficient one outside of it. Put bluntly, the same skills and personality traits that inspire others to follow your lead during surgery can rub people the wrong way the second you step outside the OR. Can you improve your ability to influence others? Of course you can. You can grow as a leader, learn new techniques, and discover new ways to influence people and move things toward the outcome you desire.

Let's return to the classroom and to the exercise I give my students. The first word I use to define effective leadership—influence—describes *what* a leader does. A leader is someone who influences others. The second word I use is *decision*. It describes *why* someone is a leader. Leaders are called to be decisive and are capable of making tough decisions. Why do *you* want to be a leader? Put another way, why is it important for you to be a leader? Leadership, after all, is a choice. Why would you make that decision? If you can understand the reasons behind your decision, you'll understand your why.

Have you ever worked for one of those "woe-is-me" leaders? Someone who complains about their responsibilities as the person in charge? You know the type. They feel burdened by their leadership status and want you to feel sorry for them and pat them on the back and say, "You're doing a good job." When someone in a position of leadership openly bemoans their duties, they're demonstrating a core fact about their leadership: They're not sure if they *want* to be a leader. In fact, it sure seems like they don't want the job. It's difficult to want to follow someone like that.

Here's a question I get all the time: Are leaders born or made? In the early twentieth century, the prevailing theory held that individuals possessed specific traits—charisma, for example—that made them natural-born leaders. More modern theories suggest that, while traits like charisma sure don't hurt, they're not sufficient to make someone a great leader. Accordingly, effective leadership requires certain skills and behaviors, all of which can be learned.

Back to that question: Are leaders born or made? My answer is both. Who you are absolutely influences the way you lead, but you can also acquire skills that you currently lack. Leadership as a decision is a powerful concept because it helps people recognize that they're making a commitment. For a leader to be accountable and engaged in their work, they must first decide to be a leader, with all its opportunities and challenges.

> Effective leadership can be boiled down to three words: influence (what a leader does), decision (why they choose to do it), and balance (how they do it).

The third term I use to define effective leadership is *balance*, which describes *how* a leader leads. We can best illustrate this point by examining leaders who are out of balance. You've probably met leaders whose leadership role dominates their life. Whether they lead a small team, a board of volunteers, or a huge corporation, they're consumed by their work at the expense of their family, friends, health, and even the job itself. Their desire to influence drives their entire life, not just their work life. As a result, they lead a life that lacks balance.

A leader who can maintain balance, on the other hand, provides a more positive role model. They're extremely effective at their job. They know when to flex their leadership and when to step back. They recognize that what works in one arena (the operating room) might not work elsewhere (the boardroom, the dining room, etc.).

Unfortunately, our culture often encourages imbalance. In the US, when we meet someone for the first time, we often ask them, "What do you do?" In other words, "How do you make a living?" Such a focus is achievement- and status-oriented. No wonder burnout and addiction are so prevalent among today's leaders. In contrast, in other countries around the world, people meeting each other for the first time might ask about each other's families or how long they've lived in the area. Such cultures place a higher premium on the art of living than on the art of accumulating wealth or climbing the corporate ladder. It's not that work and material gain are unimportant; it's just that balance makes it easier to enjoy both.

Effective leaders can balance different projects and the different needs and styles of employees. They can also balance their personal and professional life. Balance is a critical element in every choice they make.

To summarize, effective leadership can be boiled down to three words: influence (what a leader does), decision (why they choose to do it), and balance (how they do it). We opened this chapter with Brené Brown's truism that who we are is how we lead. To better understand such a notion, we had to develop a clear understanding of leadership. With that accomplished, we can turn to our next subject: the vital signs of a healthy leader.

VITAL SIGN NO. 1
PERSONAL AUTHENTICITY

Authenticity means "living your life as it was intended to be in all aspects." In *Discover Your True North*, Bill George explores the values that a healthy leader should embrace.[4] George's key message? You've got to lead from who you are and where your heart is.

The students I teach and clients I coach often try to lead like someone else. Mind you, there's nothing wrong with learning from other leaders, many of whom can inspire us to model their behavior. We notice their strengths and want to emulate them. But our first priority must be to lead from an authentic place. People recognize quickly when we're being inauthentic. If you're not naturally empathetic, for example, pretending to be so will come across as unnatural and untrue. The challenge here is to determine who you are. Who is your authentic self?

To develop your leadership compass, George tells us, you must ground your authentic self in the values that you hold. When you become aware of who you are and you interact with the world around you, you're able to be honest with yourself and others about your leadership ability. You need to spend some time thinking about your influences if you're to fully understand yourself. When you look back at your life, can you pinpoint who or what shaped your beliefs about leadership?

I grew up with a father who was a leader. He was a supervisor at a power generation station. My assumptions about leadership were shaped at an early age as I watched him and his behavior. How did he perceive himself and his employees? How did he behave? I was also fortunate enough to play for various sports teams, with each coach showing me different styles of leadership.

As an executive coach, I often ask my clients to take me through their own leadership journey, from childhood to the present. The results can be surprising. My clients learn that great leaders *and* awful ones helped shape their beliefs about leadership. Moreover, their beliefs were formed by interactions and experiences in multiple venues: the classroom, the baseball diamond, the church pew. Whether you were an Eagle Scout or a member of a social club, you likely bumped up against your share of inspiring leaders and stifling authoritarians alike. Each experience helped shape your current view of leadership.

Drawing on research from the Center for Creative Leadership (CCL) and others, George illustrates another important point: What really shapes us

> You've got to lead from who you are and where your heart is.

as leaders and has the biggest impact on us isn't just our successes but our failures. The latter George calls "crucibles of life." In such harrowing moments, when you made an error that lost the championship or when a project didn't go the way you had anticipated, you find yourself challenged on multiple levels and are forced to reexamine your thinking and priorities, among other things. Many, if not most, successful people can look back at a crisis, personal or professional—a time, for example, when they lost someone important or missed out on a job opportunity they desired—and realize that it was a turning point that ultimately helped them shape a positive future. It helped reshape and reform who they were and what they believed, ultimately shaping their core self and core values. Such "failures" are indispensable and play a critical role in every success story.

We tend to think that we learn best from success, and if you read most leadership books, they're written about someone's success. But the really interesting ones also explain where the leader failed, what they learned from that failure, and how they turned it around. Steve Jobs, for example, built a revolutionary business but had a toxic leadership style that cost him his company. Only later did he return to his business with a different orientation and perspective. History is replete with similar examples, perhaps none better than President Abraham Lincoln, who failed often but achieved things that probably no one else in his era could have accomplished. Lincoln succeeded not only because of his insights, knowledge, and grounding in spirituality, philosophy, and history but because he had learned what worked and what didn't. He learned from his failures and applied those lessons to the task ahead of him. In fact, he continued to fail throughout his career but never stopped adapting and retooling.

> One of the secrets of powerful and effective leadership is not being a perfect leader but being an authentic leader. Perfect leaders, frankly, aren't believable.

Authenticity, George tells us, is about representing to others who you actually are, not who others want you to be or who you *think* you should be. Equally important is representing to yourself who you actually are. What are your strengths? Where does your expertise lie? Where do you struggle, and where do you excel? One of the secrets of powerful and effective leadership is not being a perfect leader but being an authentic leader. Perfect leaders, frankly, aren't believable. Few of us think that anybody's *that* perfect. And most of us find it frustrating when we can't separate the truth from the many projections of an inauthentic leader. Many leaders, particularly new ones, tend to assume they must be perfect, but when they aim for perfection, they usually lose their edge. On the other hand, when they recognize their shortcomings and engage others to help them, they become more attractive as leaders and much easier to follow.

Here's a common example of inauthentic leadership: A leader knows they're supposed to seek other people's input, but they do it in a way that shows they really don't want it. They argue with it, challenge it, or disregard it instead of listening to it and using it. Such leaders often try to justify their behavior, either to themselves or others, but they know a gap exists between who they are and who they'd like to be. When we find ourselves in such a situation, the only fruitful course of action is to recognize our shortcoming and work with it. As any member of Alcoholics Anonymous would tell you, acknowledging we have a problem is the first step toward resolving it.

Try this exercise. Take a look at your life's journey and draw a simple map of what you've accomplished from your early days to today. Show those specific moments of influence, positive or negative, when you've been given an opportunity to lead or witness someone else's leadership. What did you learn? How did that moment shape you as a leader? How you were treated at one job or another likely has informed your leadership style. Maybe you learned from a great boss how to treat others. Or maybe an awful boss taught you how *not* to treat others. Tackle this exercise with a partner, whether a professional coach—i.e., someone who's prepared and does this for a living and can ask tough questions—or a trusted peer who can act as a mentor or peer coach to walk you through the steps. If you work with a peer, you'll likely both learn from the exercise.

Being an authentic leader means understanding who you are. It means recognizing your strengths and weaknesses. It means noticing that you have gaps, whether related to experience or skill, and that you entertain biases. Where are your blinders? What don't you see clearly? When you work with who you are now, in this moment, you take the first step toward being an authentic leader.

When we consider our authentic self, if we're honest with ourselves, we'll identify areas of strength and places where performance can be improved. Your authentic self is made up of both of these elements. Understanding your personal talents and the breadth of capabilities (technical and nontechnical, hard and soft skills) allows you to bring unique ideas and solutions to every interaction. They provide the lens through which you interpret and act in each situation. When recognized and refined, they become your unique superpower. We will discuss these in more detail in the next chapter. I want to briefly address the other side of the coin here.

Our willingness to acknowledge and address our own gaps is a critical step toward becoming authentic leaders. It is important to recognize and acknowledge our imperfections as leaders and as humans. The common human struggle is our effort to continually improve. In fact, a large part of the responsibility of a leader is to help others improve. We must be willing to recognize there are ways *we* can also improve—technically, socially, and as leaders. If my goal as a leader is to influence, I need to learn that it's not only my natural talents and logical arguments but how I interact with others daily that convinces others to follow. Have you ever worked for a boss who believed that every one of their opinions and or action plans was somehow divinely inspired? These types of leaders engender compliance behaviors from those they work with, not the more desired collaboration behaviors. The perception they walk above us—or more accurately, they *think* they walk above us—is a sure sign of perceptions of an inauthentic leader.

I'm not talking here about the mistakes we make in leading others but about the behaviors and habits we've developed that get in our way of being effective influencers of people. Most people will forgive our mistakes, but they judge us by the habits of our daily walk. Something as simple as consistently being late for meetings or cutting folks off in a conversation can be perceived as demonstrations that we believe our value is greater than the value of others. When these less-than-desired behavior traits become habits, they pose the greatest risk to our effectiveness as leaders. For some of us, these habits constitute addictions. Let me explain.

When we think of addictions, we tend to think of a meth addict strung out on a street corner, but addiction comes in all shapes and sizes. Addictions are those choices and/or behavioral patterns that we execute to achieve some valued reward—often without regard for their real or potential negative consequences—to self or others. Addictions eventually control us. Drugs, alcohol, gambling, food, sex, gaming, cosmetic enhancements, and social media can be sources of addiction. But so can power, control, praise, drama, chaos, validation, achievement, prestige, approval, fixing others, or success. Any driving force that takes control and begins to dictate our choices and actions might be an addiction. Some addictions are even praised in our society. Those addictions range from working eighty-hour weeks to basing our sense of value and contribution on our education, experience, or role within the organization. As is the case when attempting to address more conventional addiction risks, we must be able to recognize what presents the biggest risk to us personally and create a plan to avoid and address the risk. Sometimes we need help from a trusted friend, peer, or coach to help us identify and address our personal addiction behavior. Understanding my authentic self requires me to evaluate those things that might be controlling my life. A leader must recognize if they have addictive patterns of personal behavior, frankly, before others do—and others *will*, because they're always watching and judging the leader's behavior.

> Sharing our struggles, action plans, and progress in addressing our own challenges (even the small ones) can inspire others to find the courage to acknowledge and address their own.

You might suggest that referring to these habitual behavior patterns as addictions is hyperbole. Perhaps, but I want to impress upon you that correcting any negative behavior pattern will require that you first understand the underlying desires that are driving you, bringing into real consideration the consequences on self and others. Additionally, as a leader you might be called upon to help another. It's hard for a leader to intervene or support someone with some level of addiction when everyone knows that the leader has their own unaddressed level of addiction. Sharing our struggles, action plans, and progress in addressing our own challenges (even the small ones) can inspire others to find the courage to acknowledge and address their own. The well-known allegory from the Gospel of Matthew can serve us here: We must first remove the plank from our own eye before we can see clearly to help another remove the speck from their eye. Attempting to encourage your team toward on-time service delivery or improved accuracy when they don't see those behaviors demonstrated daily by their leader will be near impossible.

Let's take this one step further to illustrate how even such positive attributes as urgency and success can become addictions for leaders. An attending physician's role as a senior doctor accountable for overseeing patient care in a hospital or clinical setting is about managing dozens of conflicting priorities and activities. In their daily execution, often the in-the-moment urgency of the issue establishes priority. There is an addictive quality to managing workload based on urgency because it establishes a clear protocol for moving from issue to issue. Additionally, those things that fall off the plate can be explained based on requirements of higher-urgency items. When that same doctor moves to a broader leadership role, urgency still plays a critical role in time allocation. However, the definition of urgent has changed. Phone calls, emails, text messages, patient complaints—all appear urgent because they're in the moment. Attending to these items first often results in the more important tasks for the leader to fall off the plate, tasks related to strategy, crafting stakeholder communication, advancing a partnership, connecting with the administration team, etc. It can be hard to break the addiction to the urgent to invest in the important leadership tasks. It is tough for the physician transitioning out of OR roles into administrative leadership roles to break the deeply embedded urgency assumption of patient care, much less develop the willingness to delegate those urgent tasks to another.

Author Stephen Covey distinguishes between urgent and important demands. Many of us are addicted to meeting urgent demands, even when those demands are unimportant.[5] There is something satisfying about answering every call and responding to every email, because they invoke in us an urgent feeling. We feel like we're addressing the pressing issues, even when we might be letting our much more important leadership responsibility slide. Are you addicted to urgency? Try tracking your activities throughout the day, and at the end of the day, put them on a two-by-two grid that measures importance (low and high) and urgency (low and high). You will quickly see where you're spending your precious limited time. Is this an addiction you need to address? Successful physician leaders define practices to help them distinguish between the perceived urgency and actual importance of an issue. A leader might add greater value not by attending to the urgent high-profile case but by ensuring the OR schedule and staff are ready to receive such a case. Covey explains we often fail to address the important in favor of the urgent. I often remind my clients that you should be investing your time as a physician leader in those areas where *only* you can add value. These are not always the most urgent tasks but are most likely the most important.

We can also be addicted to our unique definition of success. Arthur Brooks, in his book *From Strength to Strength: Finding Success, Happiness, and Deep Purpose in the Second Half of Life*, describes how we can become addicted to the profile of success we establish for ourselves early in life and find it difficult to change later in life.[6] In our jobs and in our daily life, we come to learn what it takes to succeed. This shapes the pattern for what we expect (i.e., what behaviors are rewarded, the skills required to progress, the consequences of our actions, etc.) and what we aspire to in our work. Over time, we come to accept this definition of success. However, particularly when we change organizations and/or roles, the expectations and assumptions about what it takes to succeed change. Unfortunately, some are so addicted to the old definition of what it takes to succeed that they struggle in the new environment. The college student succeeded in studying and acquiring knowledge from books, but in the workplace, while that knowledge might inform what we do, we nevertheless must learn a new set of rules and the new conditions for success. Some skills and assumptions transfer. Others do not.

The same can be said of a worker assuming a management position. The definition of success changes. Marshall Goldsmith, a foremost leadership coach, reminds us in his book *What Got You Here Won't Get You There*, that leadership requires a different skill set than most frontline roles. He asserts that in practice, even different levels of leadership (first-line, middle manager, executive) require different perspectives and that the profile of success changes.[7] The hard part is not acquiring the new knowledge, perspectives, and skills but being willing to let go of the old ones. We have become comfortable with the status quo. Now the status quo must change. This is no easier than breaking an addiction.

As a surgeon, you might have been extremely detail-oriented, and that attention to detail set you apart and helped you become successful. But now, as you move into an environment where you're leading people on a day-to-day basis—administrators, physicians assistants, nurse practitioners, and so on—your detail-oriented mindset can work against you because you start micromanaging the people around you. Put simply, we can become attached (i.e., addicted) to the expectations, rewards, and behaviors from our previous roles, so much so that we struggle to transition to success profile of the next opportunity.

Everything I do as a leader communicates something about me as a leader. Who I am is how I lead. As we strive to be authentic in our leadership, our goal is to be real and relatable. The authentic leader starts where they are and invites others to grow with them.

VITAL SIGN NO. 2
VALUE CLARITY

Discovering your authentic self as a leader goes hand in hand with exploring your values. Your values underly your actions as a leader. They will inform (consciously or unconsciously) each discussion, each direction, each decision you make. Author and leadership expert Tara Mohr describes values as "core nutrients" to help individuals identify the essential emotional and spiritual qualities that sustain their well-being and authentic fulfillment. Drawing a parallel to physical nutrients like vitamins and minerals, Mohr encourages people to discern their unique set of core nutrients—qualities such as connection, creativity, or novelty—that are vital to their spiritual health. She guides readers and participants in her Playing Big program to reflect on past fulfilling experiences, extract the underlying qualities that made those moments nourishing, and then intentionally design their lives to ensure they receive a daily "dose" of these core nutrients.[8]

> Drawing a parallel to physical nutrients like vitamins and minerals, Mohr encourages people to discern their unique set of core nutrients—qualities such as connection, creativity, or novelty—that are vital to their spiritual health.

It's worth taking a few minutes to dig deeply to uncover your value perspectives. Create a collection of cards with a different value written on each one (you can find a list of values online), and sort them in piles of high priority, medium priority, and so forth. There's no right answer here, only *your* answer. Resist the temptation to assemble your cards according to whatever you imagine the values of a great leader happen to be. Authenticity demands that you work from your priorities, no one else's. That means some cards might not represent your values at all. Eventually, narrow your high-priority pile down to five critical values that drive you. This simple sorting forces you to identify a priority to your values—not an easy task.

As most business leaders know, there are always thousands of alternatives available to us when we're considering business objectives or strategies. The question becomes, how do we prioritize those alternatives? The same lesson applies to our values. We can adopt any number of values, especially if we're focused on what we think those values *should* be, but the point of our card exercise is to determine what our values *are*. The goal is to understand who we are, because that will shape how we lead.

> Values serve as guiding principles that influence our choices by shaping what we consider important and meaningful. They help us prioritize decisions, whether in personal relationships, careers, or ethical dilemmas.

The priorities you set will help you drive your decisions. This isn't an easy conversation, because sometimes values compete. Which is more important to you: honesty or relationships? Being ruthlessly honest could harm a relationship. Consider the physician who must determine how to deliver a difficult message to a patient and their family, who are obviously overwhelmed and frightened. The physician must weigh their personal values of accuracy and completeness against those of empathy and support. Or consider the physician leader leading through the uncertainty of a business downturn. They might have to weigh their value of being transparent about the potential of job loss against their value of not raising team anxiety prematurely.

Some values not only collide; they actually contradict each other. The exercise of prioritizing your values will help you sort that out for yourself so that you understand what your specific drivers are. For example, I believe in simplicity. I believe we, as leaders, are called to simplify. However, I also believe that to arrive at an elegant, simple answer, you often must slog through the complexity of the situation. There is no shortcut.

Honestly assessing our values and what we believe can also help us identify our personal bias and blinders. For example, in the hiring process, research has demonstrated that we often hire folks who share our preferences, who look and act as we do. Those judgments have a way of limiting creativity, inclusion, diversity of thought, ideas, and perspectives. Worse, blinders like these might reinforce the very biases and prejudices we hope to eliminate as a society. Part of being authentic is recognizing our biases. Only when we recognize them can we choose to overcome them.

Values serve as guiding principles that influence our choices by shaping what we consider important and meaningful. They help us prioritize decisions, whether in personal relationships, careers, or ethical dilemmas. Strong values lead to consistent and purpose-driven decision-making, aligning actions with our core beliefs. As suggested, there is virtually no limit to the values that might serve as a core and grounding element in your life.

Since this book is about leadership, let's explore one set of values in more detail: the role of work in our lives. What values drive your beliefs and behavior related to how you integrate work into your life (i.e., your work-life balance)?

Some of us are addicted to work. In fact, many in our society consider working late or spending our weekends at the office a badge of honor. We brag about pulling another seventy-hour work week or working another ten-hour shift. A zealous-value focus on work at the expense of the rest of life appears to be cultural. Not all cultures value work the same way that Americans have historically. For the baby boomers, the value of work topped almost every other value. I'm embarrassed to share that when I was starting a new job, I left my wife and our five-day-old son at home in Pittsburgh in three feet of snow because my work called for me to travel to Australia for two weeks. In the US, I see a shift occurring among the younger generations, who seem to have a keener understanding of the balance of things. Baby boomers and Generation X tend to let the job dominate, but millennials and Gen Z are seeking value elsewhere.

In any case, I've never liked the term *work-life balance*, if only because work is a part of life. Using the phrase suggests a strange dichotomy in which life is everything but work. In reality, many of us find social engagement and gain a sense of belonging and accomplishment through work, not in spite of it. If we return to our definition of a leader—someone who influences, makes decisions, and strives for balance—we can see that leaders must grapple with difficult decisions when it comes to finding balance between work, family, play, and so forth, not only for themselves but for those they lead.

A lot of well-intentioned leaders and HR departments try to implement a work-life balance program to help employees, but I would argue that a better strategy would be to manage our addiction to work. Why do we need to work eighty hours a week? Sure, some of us have jobs that require long hours or go through seasons that require a lot of overtime. A physician in a residency program has no control over their time because of the nature of their accountability on the job, but hopefully once finished, they can exert more control. Must they keep on working those long hours? A client of mine is retiring soon, and he still demonstrates the same kind of addiction to work that he did as a resident. People moving away from work face an enormous challenge: how to fill that void. If we break life into its different components—family, work, friends, social engagements, charitable activities, and so on—we can view moving into retirement as a simple shift in those components. But if we're addicted to the patterns of work, retirement becomes a crisis. We don't know how to change our definition of success.

Years ago, I had a boss who told me he wanted me to work no more than forty hours a week—a fine idea, but one that failed to consider the project I had been tasked with completing. I ended up working forty hours at the office and then another X number of hours at home. I *had* to, or I would fall behind. Well-meaning bosses will tell employees about to go on vacation, "Leave your laptop at home," or "Don't answer calls." But for some employees, that results in an imbalance, not balance. Balancing everything in your life is a distinctly individual act, which is why, when we try to prescribe for others how they should balance their lives, we often add to their burden rather than relieve it. I don't go anywhere without my laptop, not because I'm using it all the time but because I need to know it's available if I need it. Bottom line? Your balance and my balance might look very different, and that's okay.

Even work that is meaningful and important can become an addiction. We can see as much in the high level of burnout, alcoholism, drug use, and other addictions among highly successful health-care professionals. Doctors, nurses, and other health-care providers are making an enormous contribution to others and to society, but often they haven't invested time in themselves. Many become addicted to work and neglect their physical, emotional, and spiritual health. Brian Dyson, CEO at Coca-Cola from 1986 to 1991, delivered a short speech at Georgia Tech's 172nd commencement on September 6, 1991, sharing this brilliant metaphor that remains frequently quoted to this day:

> *Imagine life as a game in which you are juggling some five balls in the air. You name them work, family, health, friends, and spirit. And you're keeping all of these in the air. You will soon understand that work is a rubber ball. If you drop it, it will bounce back. But the other four balls—family, health, friends, and spirit—are made of glass. If you drop one of these, they*

will be irrevocably scuffed, marked, nicked, damaged, or even
shattered. They will never be the same. You must understand
that and strive for balance in your life.[9]

We can't be authentic without determining what our values are
and what we believe and then striving to align our actions with them.

VITAL SIGN NO. 3
EMOTIONAL INTELLIGENCE

Emotional intelligence (EQ) refers to the ability to recognize, understand, manage, and influence your own emotions and to recognize, understand, and influence the emotions of others. You'll notice that I left out the word *manage* in the second half of the definition. We can't manage the emotions of others, although we *can* influence them.[10]

We can break down emotional intelligence into four key components. The first two relate to understanding and managing your own emotions, and the second two relate to understanding and influencing the emotions of others.

1. **Self-awareness:** accurately recognizing your own emotions.
2. **Self-regulation:** being able to control your emotional responses and apply the appropriate emotional response to the situation.
3. **Empathy:** being able to connect with someone else's emotions, to understand and consider their emotions as a valid element within the social setting and situation.
4. **Relationship management:** recognizing and managing emotions within our relationships. Emotions have a dramatic impact on our ability to build networks and maintain relationships.

Let's contrast emotional intelligence with the different types of intelligence. The most common measurement of intelligence is IQ, which is the intelligence quotient. IQ is an age-related measurement of cognitive abilities. It's our ability to logically reason and explain our capacity for basic learning, which correlates highly with academic performance. When we account for age, this measurement is fairly static over our lifetimes.

Social intelligence is being able to effectively interpret social interactions. Social intelligence overlaps with EQ in awareness of emotions in self and others but also includes other factors involved in interpreting social situations to craft responses.

Cultural intelligence, CQ, is the ability to work effectively across cultures and adapt to different behavioral patterns in individuals that can be influenced by culture. Culture influences our emotions and reactions and those of others.

In contrast to these other metrics of intelligence, EQ is developmental, meaning that it's not static. It can be built. It can grow over time. We can learn to have a higher emotional intelligence as we learn to recognize emotions in ourselves and others. Additionally, it grows when we learn how to exert control over our emotions and recognize the influence of our emotions (intended or unintended) on others.

Social and cultural intelligence influence our EQ and vice versa. While IQ is not related directly to our level of EQ, in practice often high-IQ individuals who are excellent at acquiring information and applying logic to identify solutions—demonstrate lower levels of EQ. The reliance on facts, analysis, and logical explanations can result in downplaying or overlooking the emotional elements of a situation. Most of my EQ work as a leadership coach has been with highly intelligent individuals.

Consider the physician who's so focused on the diagnosis and treatment of an ailment of their patient that they don't recognize the impact their delivery of the facts and treatment plan have on the patient. Part of maintaining a good bedside manner is shaping the discussion in a way that recognizes how the patient and family are receiving the information. The doctor who flies into the room to deliver difficult news without taking the time to build the rapport and trust with the stakeholders, without recognizing the anxiety of the patient, might feel they have accurately explained the situation, but the perceptions of their approach and the emotions of the stakeholder are shouting louder than the message delivered. I know doctors who ensure up front that they have the opportunity to visit with the family and invest in rapport development. They recognize that for many patients this situation and relationship might be *the* most critical one in their life at this moment of illness. This is a demonstration of high EQ.

A leader with high emotional intelligence also demonstrates self-awareness of how they impact other people—how their voice inflection, their tone, the rate of their speech, their facial gestures, and their body language are communicating emotional clues. They understand that others are using these clues, not just the leader's words, to interpret situations. An emotional leader will also have empathy for other people and recognize the verbal and nonverbal cues in someone else that might demonstrate either anger, frustration, or anxiety, even when they don't express their emotions verbally. The leader without EQ behaves like *Dragnet* detective Joe Friday at a crime scene: "Just the facts, ma'am. Just the facts." High EQ leaders understand that emotions are facts. They train themselves to listen and watch for not just the facts of a situation or the logical content but also the emotional content. They understand emotions shape meaning and the relationships being built.

> High EQ leaders listen and watch for not just the facts of a situation or the logical content but also the emotional content. They understand emotions shape meaning and the relationships being built.

So how do we build emotional intelligence as individuals? EQ is built upon self-awareness. To be self-aware, we need feedback. We need to understand how others see us. How we're perceived by others is shaped by their reactions to our behaviors. Yes, their perceptions are filtered through their unique lens, but the only thing we can control is our behavior, not their biases or judgments. We need to ask for and listen to others' feedback. One effective tool for collecting these perceptions is a 360-degree assessment, which you can use to actively seek feedback from different stakeholders in your world (e.g., boss, peers, direct reports, others). This rounded feedback allows you to learn not only if there are patterns others see in your behavior; it also helps you see if you're perceived differently by different stakeholder groups. Your team might share that you come across as curt and dismissive, while your boss might not experience you the same way.

> Nothing will damage your impact as a leader more than allowing your emotions to control you instead of you controlling them.

Interesting feedback. There are formal 360 tools available online and via HR departments that can gather feedback for you on specific target competencies. There are also less formal ways to gather this 360-degree feedback. Ask those around you what you should start, stop, or continue. It can help to ask this in a way that protects your team's anonymity (i.e., online via a survey tool) so members feel free to give you specific feedback. I will share from personal experience that 360-degree feedback can be very enlightening. I learned that my exuberance and excitement can for some be perceived as frustration or even anger as I dig into and challenge ideas—never my intent, but an important lesson for me to hear. Learning this allowed me to work on my self-regulation of those behaviors.

Self-regulation is no easy task. We like to think that emotions are natural and spontaneous. Well, the emotion might be. How we choose to express it is not. Understanding our hot buttons is an important first step in self-regulation. Knowing what will trigger us allows us to not only avoid those situations but also to have a practiced response in place when the blood pressure starts to rise or drop. Mindfulness techniques, deep breathing, journaling, and the five-second rule are all examples of self-regulation. Simply pausing five seconds before you respond often allows you to take control and choose how to react in a stressful situation. Sometimes being a leader comes with great disappointment or frustration. Nothing will damage your impact as a leader more than allowing your emotions to control you instead of you controlling them. Feedback like "You wear your emotions on your sleeve" or "Your expression gives you away" suggests we need to work on our self-regulation. "You never seem rattled" might be feedback that you're on the right track. We all need coping strategies. Perhaps calling for a short break or taking a walk can help. In his book *Positive Intelligence*, Shirzad Chamine describes how simple actions like slow breathing, lightly rubbing two fingers together to feel the ridges on each finger, or attempting to count each toe during a stressful situation uses our sensory capabilities to distract our brain, break the negative cycle, and redirect our emotions to more positive expressions.[11]

To build emotional intelligence, we must also build empathy. Empathy involves understanding and sharing another's feelings. Sympathy, in contrast, is feeling concern for someone's situation without necessarily experiencing their emotions. So, to be empathic, we must learn perspective-taking, which is practicing seeing situations from other people's perspective. What would the patient be thinking right now when I'm about to share with them a significant diagnosis? What might the surgical team be feeling now before we debrief a case that didn't produce the desired outcome? A second really important skill in building empathy is active listening, which is being able to fully focus and fully attune to someone else's thoughts, ideas, and perspectives—being able to listen without (pre)judgment. Stephen Covey suggests that one of the seven habits of highly effective people is to "seek first to understand."[12] To learn empathy, I need to practice listening.

A third skill in building emotional intelligence is being a conflict-competent leader. We'll address conflict resolution in more detail later, but for now, consider the importance of staying calm and seeking win-win solutions whenever possible. As leaders, we're not only accountable for resolving conflict that involves us; we're also responsible to ensure the team knows how to resolve conflict in productive ways. Leaders can develop the social skills of conflict resolution by ensuring mutual respect and highlighting mutual goals.

How do we build emotional intelligence in our team? Perhaps you've noticed that some members of your team don't recognize the emotional impact they have on others. Others might not recognize (or care) when someone else is anxious, disconnected, angry, or frustrated. As leaders, we can make a space for team members to self-reflect. We can call them to consider the impact their actions, behaviors, and emotions have on others. By providing the space for this consideration, we validate the importance of emotions and their impact within effective collaboration.

Secondly, providing a culture of feedback is critical. You need to seek feedback to be self-aware. As leaders, we must seek and consider feedback. When we model the behavior of listening, self-awareness, and self-regulation, we're teaching the team. We can model ways to express emotions in positive and appropriate ways.

Team members might need your help developing their own coping skills to support their self-regulation. They'll definitely need your protection when emotions are expressed in an inappropriate way. Emotions are a part of every conversation, and they're a part of almost every social activity. So as leaders, we must learn to recognize and regulate our own behaviors and help others do the same.

VITAL SIGN NO. 4
GRATITUDE ATTITUDE

Consider what it's like to work for a boss who engages in gossip or regularly accuses or condemns members of their team, encouraging an environment of insecurity and backbiting. Now imagine working for someone who daily demonstrates an "attitude of gratitude" and infectious positivity that spreads to the whole team. Which boss do you want to work for? A culture of gratitude starts at the top with a leader who leads by example. It encourages teamwork, accountability, and positive momentum toward mission outcomes.

Research demonstrates that those who follow a regular gratitude practice will enjoy physical, emotional, and spiritual benefits.[13] Gratitude—being thankful, appreciating others, recognizing kindness and generosity—has a direct impact on those who demonstrate it and those who receive it. If you're a leader, or a prospective one, your decision to show gratitude to your organization and the people who comprise it will have a profound impact on you and everyone around you.

> Research demonstrates that those who follow a regular gratitude practice will enjoy physical, emotional, and spiritual benefits.

Those with more gratitude demonstrate higher levels of life satisfaction, sleep better, and come back quicker and more easily from trauma while suffering less from anxiety, crises, and burnout. Gratitude literally rewires our brains, moving us from a reactionary attitude to one of empathy and compassion. Consistently practicing gratitude creates new neural pathways and strengthens existing ones and can lead to long-lasting changes in brain structure and function. The results include: more positive emotions, better emotional regulation, a greater sense of well-being, and even improved memory recall.

Better still, gratitude promotes adaptive coping strategies and personal resilience. Grateful people better recognize their strengths while showing more self-compassion. They can maintain a more positive and balanced perspective, even during challenging times. They're more likely to experience joy and contentment, glean positive life lessons, seek social support, and bond with others. They experience pain less intensely and even enjoy better heart health. And they pass through those crucibles of life explored earlier with more equanimity.

When you cultivate an attitude of gratitude in your leadership role, it enhances team morale, strengthens relationships, and ultimately contributes to a more engaged and motivated workforce.

I recently spoke with a clinician who, while reviewing his career history, shared a story about not getting a health-care administrator/chair role in his department. At the time, he was disappointed and frustrated. But now, ten years later, he looks back at that moment and feels grateful he "failed." He wasn't ready for the promotion, he realizes now, and likely would have struggled in the new role, which could have had a negative impact on his career. Most of us, when we reevaluate our career trajectories, can point to moments when all felt lost at the time. Now those moments look almost serendipitous. They look that way because we're viewing them through the lens of gratitude.

So what, precisely, is a gratitude practice, and how can we implement one in our life? In its simplest form, a gratitude practice constitutes any habit or ritual—ideally a daily one—that connects us to the positive aspects of our lives. Perhaps the easiest habit to implement is journal writing. Your life will begin to look different if you pick up a journal three times a week or once a day and express your gratitude for something or someone. Try it. See what happens to your attitude after making just a few entries.

As leaders, we can help our organizations practice gratitude in a variety of ways, from simple exercises to more complicated rituals. We can assemble our team and form a gratitude exchange, encouraging each member to express their gratitude about someone or something, work-related or not. We can organize a ritual like a thirty-day gratitude challenge, during which everyone is encouraged to take a moment every day for thirty days to name something that inspires their gratitude. Another simple gratitude practice is an affirmation walk, where we focus on a different recipient of gratitude for every block we walk, simply listing something or someone we are grateful for as we travel from place to place.

Practicing gratitude is about more than being nice. It's more than simply saying, "Please," and "Thank you," although a good leader does both every day. Consider carving out an hour and a half of your time to listen to Andrew Huberman's podcast entitled "The Science of Gratitude and How to Build a Gratitude Practice."[14] As Huberman points out, you can give, receive, and observe gratitude. And according to research, even the mere act of observing someone else demonstrating gratitude confers evidence-based emotional, physical, and spiritual benefits upon the observer.

Perhaps one of the greatest impacts of the regular expression of gratitude is that it can completely revitalize relationships. No other activity builds bridges like recognizing and expressing genuine gratitude for the talents, perspectives, and accomplishments of others. When you express your gratefulness to me for something specific I did, large or small, it demonstrates you noticed and valued my contribution. Gratitude is known to melt the hard heart and to open eyes to the perspective of others. Gratitude can be a powerful tool when used in a leadership role. Genuine gratitude comes from a place of authenticity and sincerity. When you cultivate an attitude of gratitude in your leadership role, it enhances team morale, strengthens relationships, and ultimately contributes to a more engaged and motivated workforce.

There are many prompts and expressions of gratitude. One powerful prompt is music. Its melodic patterns/themes, poetic words, and joy in performance can stir strong emotions deep within our souls. Music is unique in human experience and its impact on the human brain. Its multidimensional nature allows it to stimulate and calm, engage and repeal, challenge and comfort. Music can be experienced alone, within a relationship, or with a large group (of almost any size). It can be enjoyed in the foreground or the background. In *I Heard There Was a Secret Chord*, Daniel J. Levitin explores how music functions as one of humanity's oldest and most effective forms of medicine, drawing on neuroscience and global traditions to demonstrate music's profound impact on healing and well-being.[15] Levitin explains how music therapy can alleviate symptoms of conditions like Parkinson's, Alzheimer's, depression, and chronic pain. He also illuminates the mysterious ways music connects to memory, movement, and emotional health. Gratitude, like music, engages several parts of the brain to bring comfort, confidence, and joy.

Gratitude, just like authenticity, values, and emotional intelligence (EQ), plays a critical role in leadership. If you want to get the most out of yourself and those you lead, you'll make time to express and explore gratitude every day. The more you show, receive, and observe, the more you'll benefit.

PREVENTIVE HEALTH ACTIONS (2-DO'S)
ACTIONS TO TAKE TO ENSURE HEART HEALTH.

Invest in yourself as a leader. The best investment you can make for your team is developing yourself as a leader. The more you know about who you are, the better leader you will be. The more you understand your strengths, your biases, your values, your beliefs, the stronger leader you will become. Engage in personal reflection, and/or seek out a coach. Consider doing some coursework—whatever helps you build a greater understanding of yourself. Books and podcasts are also great resources.

Develop a gratitude practice. Start by taking note of the people and things in your life that inspire gratitude: your family, friends, health, job, and so forth. Do this three times a week, and personalize the exercise—i.e., do it in a way that works best for you. You can keep a gratitude journal or engage in a practice called "the three benefits," identifying three benefits in every situation, negative or positive. Or you can implement a gratitude ritual, like beginning every meeting with an expression of gratitude. Keep a list of individuals to whom you wish to express your gratitude. Or take the thirty-day gratitude challenge and express your gratitude for someone or something once every day for the next thirty days. You can use mindfulness, yoga, and music to build your gratitude practice. And whenever negativity threatens your thinking, recognize it, acknowledge it, and then balance it with your gratitude practice.

For additional resources to support you on these vital signs, visit vitalsigns-book/resources.

As a physician leader, I stay engaged by remembering the incredible privilege it is to do this work. We're invited into the most personal and vulnerable moments of people's lives—births, crises, recovery. That kind of thing calls me to show up every day committed to being better. Whether it's improving efficiency, patient care, or staff experience, I see engagement as a form of respect for the people we serve.

I stay personally engaged by investing time and presence in the people I lead. I don't just focus on outcomes. I attend to emotions, relationships, and community. Every quarter, I host gatherings at my home because I want my residents and faculty to see me not just as their leader but as someone who genuinely cares for them.

—Summary of interview with a physician leader: Residency Director, ENT

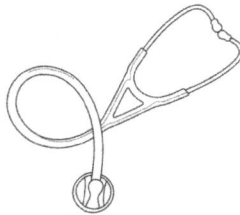

The E-ngaged Leader

"Leadership is the capacity to translate vision into reality."
—Warren Bennis

PRESENTING SYMPTOMS ADDRESSED IN THIS CHAPTER

Decreased job satisfaction.	Career stagnation.
Feelings of disengagement.	Increased stress.
Feelings of frustration.	Bored.
Strained relationships.	Loss of influence.

B ack when I was an undergraduate student working for a power generation station, two different managers of two different engineering maintenance departments demonstrated a fundamental lesson about what it means to be an engaged leader.

The first manager would assign his team members various tasks and then check on their status at the end of each day. He didn't seem particularly emotionally invested in the mission, and he often complained about the work. Likely you've seen this kind of thing before: In his view, the challenge was always too great, the timeline too short, and the resources too thin. Even as a college student, it only took one summer for it to become clear to me that most people didn't want to work for this leader; they wanted to work for his counterpart.

The second manager always made it clear that he found the work challenging and interesting. He built a reputation for being a problem solver and leader who encouraged, enriched, and challenged his team to do more. He never accepted that something couldn't be done, and instead always devised creative ideas to help his team accomplish their goals. As a result, the organization started to depend on his ingenuity. Eventually, all of the more challenging, interesting, and time- and/or resource-critical projects went to his team. Unlike his counterpart, he embraced these changes with open arms. He must have walked ten miles a day on the job. He was constantly moving from one project to another, connecting with his team members, and committing to the hard work and critical thinking that each project required. He always had his teams engaged and challenged as a result.

It is the leader's responsibility to turn the day-to-day activities of their employees into action that advances the organization's vision. This responsibility—to become, if you will, what leadership studies pioneer Dr. Warren Bennis calls the bridge between dreams and tangible results—requires you to be much more than just a manager who tells people what to do. You must become an *engaged* leader, someone who has made the conscious decision to be actively involved, absorbed in, and committed to not only the mission of an organization but to the *role* of being a leader.

People are motivated to become leaders for different reasons. Some see leadership as a means to an end (for example, to accomplish certain career objectives, to enjoy a broader scope of responsibility and visibility, or to receive higher pay). Others view it as a destination unto itself. They aspire to be a leader because of their natural interest and ability in empowering and engaging other people.

Ironically, whether you're a surgeon, an accountant, or a ditch-digger, the more you develop your skills within your respective role, the more likely you are to be asked to lead a team, which requires mastering a completely *different* set of skills. The best employee usually gets promoted to manager, which in practical terms means the best welder gets promoted to run the welding crew. Sometimes that works great. Many times it doesn't, because being a high-level tradesperson or high-level academic or a high-level clinician is very different from being an effective and engaged leader. Further, as Marshall Goldsmith explains, when we move up or across the organizational ladder into different leadership roles, our responsibilities change.[16] What all of this means is that leadership requires not only a different set of skills, but different behaviors and accountabilities as well. Often, it also requires a different perspective.

As always, to find that perspective, we begin by turning the search inward and checking your vitals as a physician leader.

VITAL SIGN NO. 1
PROFESSIONAL CURIOSITY

An engaged leader is a curious leader. An unengaged leader does not demonstrate curiosity about leadership, about outcomes, about the characteristics and responsibilities of a leader, or about how to make their organization better. They're simply not motivated to make the kinds of decisions necessary to improve their leadership and their organization.

The first job of a curious leader is to understand what motivates them to lead. Why do you *want* to be a leader? After all, leadership is hard. It requires different skills than you've used to become so successful as a physician. It can be emotionally taxing, highly stressful, and ultimately frustrating because you're trying to get work done by enlisting other people in that work. Why would you want to do that?

Traditionally, leadership was viewed as the next rung on the career ladder. But today, more and more organizations realize that there are many ways to contribute and that not everyone has the skills, interests, or capability to be an effective leader. So let's consider the question one more time. Why do you want to be a leader? Maybe it's for recognition and status. Maybe career advancement motivates you: better compensation, better opportunities. It's true: Leaders typically enjoy higher status and are more visible in an organization, and some of us aspire to that. We like the recognition and prestige that comes with leadership. Of course, a self-serving motivation can lead a person to become invested in their own outcomes but not necessarily the organization's outcomes. People typically see through the self-motivated leader.

Some people want leadership because of the challenges associated with it. When you become a leader, you're often given challenging projects. You're granted the opportunity to not only tackle them yourself but to enlist other resources in the task. It's a bit of a chess game. It moves from using an individual strategy to considering multiple strategies that require thoughtful contemplation. Many of us derive joy from overcoming those kinds of challenges and contributing to success.

Maybe you want to be a leader because it benefits your personal growth and your legacy and long-term impact. If that's the case, your own motivations aren't the only ones to consider. Are you interested in becoming a leader because you have a passion for the organization's mission? Perhaps you have a passion for leading and inspiring other people. If you have a gift for bringing groups together to collaborate, to influence others, or to encourage and challenge individuals to aim for higher performance, you can help make a positive impact and seek leadership roles to contribute to an organization, your community, or society at large.

> The first job of a curious leader is to understand what motivates them to lead. Why do you *want* to be a leader?

If you're curious about your personal motivation to be a leader, you will strive to understand the difference between what truly inspires you and what you think *ought* to inspire you. Most of us, it turns out, are inspired to become leaders for multiple reasons. The more you understand what's driving you, the more you can balance not only your internal motivation but your alignment with the organization's mission and the accountabilities of a leader.

If we're unsure about our motivations and passions or have thus far made decisions without first exploring our personal reasons for aspiring to leadership, we have a readymade treatment available to us: *ikigai*. A Japanese word, ikigai means a reason for being. Why do you get up in the morning? The ikigai process represents a holistic approach to help find purpose and fulfillment in your life. To better understand our purpose, our unique fit in life, it calls us each to ask the following four questions:

1. **What's your passion?** Explore which activities/pursuits bring you joy, satisfaction, and a sense of fulfillment.
2. **What are you really good at?** Take a look at your strengths, talents, and skills—all those areas in which you excel and for which you earn recognition.
3. **What does the world need?** Consider what your work community or society at large needs that's related to your passion and skills. Then take a look at how you can meet that need and give back.
4. **Lastly, what can you be paid for?** Find out what vocation best suits you. Search for opportunities for a career or a vocation that reflects your passion and skills.

When you put these four questions together, you have what you love (your passions), what you're good at (your skills), what the world needs (your mission), and what you can be paid for (your vocation). With those in mind, you can create a Venn diagram that illustrates where all four intersect. As you'll see, you're uniquely positioned to accomplish objectives, and by understanding how your passions, skills, mission, and vocation overlap, you have all the motivation you need to engage your pursuits as a leader on a day-to-day basis. At first, this might apply on a broad level, such as medical doctor, but as you continue to refine these four questions, it can help you further define your unique contribution, such as an academic physician or surgeon with a clinical practice and research lab focused on pediatric otolaryngology. Perhaps you'll see that at this stage in your life you aspire to make a contribution as a clinical leader or practice leader, engaging others in the pursuit of a defined mission.

> To truly be engaged in our work, we will be curious.

To truly be engaged in our work, we will be curious. We will want to learn as much as possible about the business and its unique value proposition(s). Why did it start? How has it changed over time? What services/products are delivered? How do our customers feel about our services/products? What characteristics do our customers share? How do we make money? What reputation have we built in the community? There is no end to the questions an engaged worker might ask to build a connection to the organization and its mission. To truly be engaged in our work *as a leader*, we will be curious. We will want to learn as much as we can about not only our organization but also the people we lead. Why did they join the team? What are the unique skills and capabilities each member brings to the team? What motivates each member? How do our customers view our team? How do members of the team view our team? How has the team changed over time? The questions a leader might ask to build connections across their team are almost endless.

Being curious about ourselves, our team, and our organization is the secret to being an engaged leader.

VITAL SIGN NO. 2
MISSION AND VISION

Organizations have mission statements. Do you have a mission statement? Have you taken the time to define for yourself, in your profession and as a leader, your stated mission? A **mission statement** is a concise declaration of an organization's or individual's purpose, core values, and goals. It defines what they do, who they serve, and how they aim to make an impact. Considering your personal mission is an important step to being a HEART-healthy leader. A strong mission statement provides direction, motivation, and a framework for decision-making. Just like in organizations, once a mission is defined, the paths to reaching that mission can be shaped and evaluated. Organizations and individuals that lack a clear purpose and goals often waste precious time and energy chasing whatever fad or fancy is currently popular.

It's hard to make clear decisions when you don't know your *Why*. Simon Sinek in his book, *Start with Why*, describes what he calls the "Golden Circle," which has three layers.[17] The inner most circle is the *Why* and describes the purpose that drives action. The *How* circle surrounds the *Why* circle and describes the actions required to fulfill the *Why*. And the outermost circle is the *What*, which includes the products/services delivered as a result of the actions. Sinek argues that people are drawn to organizations, products, and leaders that communicate their *Why* first, creating deeper trust, loyalty, and long-term success. Your mission statement defines your *Why*. As a physician, an architect, or a bricklayer, you should have a *Why* related to your mission in your profession. Leaders also need to consider their *Why* in deciding to be a leader. Although your motivations for being a leader are different than your purpose, you might find clues in the considerations of the last vital sign to help you articulate your personal mission.

I strongly recommend you create for yourself a personal mission statement. It might cover a broader scope than just your profession (i.e., mother, daughter, educator, etc.) but should articulate your life's purpose. Even more than the final words themselves, the process of reflection is of great value and will serve you daily. The mission can focus attention and inspire creativity. How can we best deliver against the goals of this mission? Once a life mission is defined (i.e., what you do), you can better focus attention on defining your vision of the future (i.e., what you hope to achieve and how).

Richard Boyatzis, a distinguished professor at Case Western Reserve University, has produced an interesting set of studies related to brain activity using brain scans when we engage in various activities. He noted that brain activity increases significantly when we use our imagination. When we allow ourselves to envision future possibilities, when we're thinking about what could be and about potential opportunities and alternatives, when we're building, creating, and thinking about broad things, brain activity increases dramatically. Therefore, Boyatzis, encourages leaders to engage their imaginations, to utilize as much brain power as possible, and to energize and engage themselves in the work of fulfilling a mission.

> A mission statement is a concise declaration of an organization's or individual's purpose, core values, and goals.

Rather than narrowly focusing on the here and now, which is often recommended by executive coaches during development discussions (e.g., What three specific behaviors do you want to develop during our engagement? What will you accomplish before our next session?), Boyatzis encourages the exploration of the concept of the "ideal self" as a critical part of personal development. The ideal self is that vivid, personal vision of the person you aspire to become, encompassing your deepest values, purpose, dreams, and hopes. The ideal self serves as a core driver for intentional change by providing motivation, direction, and personal engagement that help individuals focus on their aspirations and guide their growth toward meaningful, sustained transformation. By engaging the energy of our brain, we can begin to define what our desired future will look like and determine possible paths to move toward it.

Since hearing Boyatzis speak, I've made a habit of starting each engagement with my clients with a "Define your ideal life" exercise. Consider fifteen years into the future. What would you like your life to look like? We talk about relationships; physical, spiritual, and mental health; career goals; engagement in societal activities and other aspirations. Boyatzis usually recommends projecting out by fifteen years, but if you're older or approaching the end of your career, you can shorten the timeline as needed. But this is a long-term envisioning process. The idea is to clearly paint the target you're trying to hit and by when. Boyatzis's research shows that we're more engaged, more interested, and more committed while imagining those things that energize us in the long term than we are while addressing the details of the short term. As leaders, we can get lost in the details. We're always called to be putting out fires, but we need to allow ourselves to dream and articulate our ideal future. Short-term details are still important, of course, but since we're talking about assessing and developing your engagement as a leader, challenge yourself to take the time to think about what the ideal life looks like for you. How does being a leader fit into that vision?

> The ideal self serves as a core driver for intentional change by providing motivation, direction, and personal engagement that help individuals focus on their aspirations and guide their growth toward meaningful, sustained transformation.

Perhaps part of your ideal future is to be leading a larger organization, moving from a primary care delivery position into a leader of a practice, or moving from being a team member assigned to a project to managing future projects. Perhaps you aspire to political service or other types of engagement. The personal growth challenge here is to figure out how leadership fits into your ideal life. Maybe you want to reach a certain stage of experience or expertise, or maybe you want to be the CEO of a company or land a global assignment. Regardless, you need to establish what your ideal life is and plan accordingly. Leadership, as we referenced at the beginning of this chapter, is moving from vision to reality.

When someone has defined an ideal life, it reframes not only their long-term plans but also short-term decisions. With a clear ideal (goal) in mind, we can approach each decision by considering how various alternatives help us move toward that defined ideal. In this sense, each day and each decision should bring us a little closer to our desired objective. I find this orientation helps clients consider the important matters of career decisions, project choices, development assignments, investments, and a host of other pressing life issues. Such an approach reminds us of the current priority and ultimate desired outcome and ensures that neither gets lost in the daily grind.

Considering longer-term goals also highlights investments that must be made (e.g., education, experiences) and helps us anticipate the trade-offs (job changes, financial risks) that must be made to achieve our goal. Over time, our ideal life will evolve as some things become higher priorities and others that were once primary concerns fade. I recommend that leaders reconsider their ideal life at least annually. It's an excellent exercise at the end of the year to look back and see what progress has been made (or not) toward your ideal life during that year. Opportunities taken, opportunities lost. Then you can more effectively turn your eyes and energy toward the future.

The idea and energy of the ideal life can be applied to smaller, more immediate plans as well. What would the ideal leader look like? How do individual actions move me closer to demonstrating the behaviors of an ideal leader? What is the ideal life for the team I lead? How should this team work together to provide maximum value and satisfaction for the team members? This conversation within the team is rich and stimulates the brain power of the team. Once established, team decisions can be weighed within the context of what moves us closer to our defined ideal. Sure, sometimes we need to take detours on our journey, but too often we accept the path available (status quo) rather than blaze the trail that takes us more directly toward our desired destination. An engaged leader is a trailblazer removing the obstacles in the way of the desired future.

Let's stop to consider what you think an ideal leader looks like. Perhaps you've had some military experience, or maybe you have an MBA. Such experiences help inform what leadership means for you. Maybe you've read about a great leader or you've seen one in action who has shaped your assumptions about what it takes to be a great leader. Some new leaders scour the literature to learn about each leadership theory (i.e., transformational, servant, situational) and its applications.

I once attended an amazing weeklong workshop on organizational diagnosis that was designed to help us as consultants learn how to recognize and address issues within the organization. I anticipated we would jump in and examine the various scholarly models of dissecting and organization. We did not. Instead, the facilitator asked us to define visually and in words our own model of how organizations worked. What were the major assumptions, variables, processes, and constraints that influenced effective operation within an organization? How were they interconnected? We spent three full days of a five-day workshop each defining our own model. Then we spent the last two days discussing those academic models that I was so eager to explore. The question posed to us as we discussed each popular theory was this: How does this theory enhance or modify *your* model of organizations? The instructor taught me a priceless lesson: Explore first what you believe; then enhance with the perspective of others.

For most of us, such an approach to learning is foreign. We're more comfortable with beginning learning with the lessons learned from others. Here we're talking about the difference between pedagogy (how children are taught) and andragogy (how adults should be taught). Pedagogy assumes that the learner has no context for the subject and attempts

> Explore first what you believe; then enhance with the perspective of others.

to build, block by block, the context and skills required. Andragogy, on the other hand, is aimed at experienced learners. Adults typically have a context for most subjects learned through trial and error, watching others, and of course, pedagogical experiences (school).

As adults outside a formal instructional environment, we still learn. In fact, just like my two-year-old granddaughter, we learn from every experience, including our successes and failures. Adult learning means connecting new experiences with those that already exist within our memory/experience bank. As an adult, you have seen plenty of leaders. You have a context for leadership. You have beliefs about what makes a good leader and what derails them. Teaching a graduate-level class in leadership is a far different experience than teaching high-school students. Typically, the graduate students, particularly students already in the workforce, have a context for leaders that is meaningful and valuable to them and that they use to evaluate the class material.

Reviewing leadership theory to understand concepts and applications is helpful, but I encourage you to first consider your beliefs, experiences, and ideas on a subject. Never base your opinion solely on someone else's input. Your organization might have a set of competencies, models, and behaviors that it expects from its leaders. How does that integrate with your vision of the ideal leader? By the way, that model I created and then refined in that five-day workshop twenty years ago still hangs in my office and influences my work today.

From your experience, is there a best way to lead? Certainly, there are bad, unproductive ways to lead. A disengaged leader, a berating leader, a micromanaging leader—such leaders exhibit behaviors that are traditionally associated with bad leadership. But as you'll remember from chapter 1, leadership is about being authentic, and part of being authentic is understanding your own perspective on leadership.

I once consulted with a nonprofit organization that was discussing how to transition from one leader to the next. The original founder of the nonprofit had served in the military and worked from assumptions of command and control. The incoming leader, meanwhile, held assumptions that reflected a more inclusive, distributive approach to leadership. The transition caused a lot of angst in the organization because no one could agree on the best way to lead.

While most HR departments and even some MBA programs might claim to know the right way to lead, I would argue simply that there are more effective ways and less effective ways to be a leader. Part of finding the more effective way for you is to understand your basic assumptions about leadership. What do you assume about its accountabilities, authority, empowerment, and relationship with employees?

Some people assume that you can't be friends with your employees *and* be a good leader. Others say that to be a good leader, you *must* be friends with them. What do you believe about this? What have you observed in various organizations? What behaviors do the leaders you respect demonstrate? What styles and methods do they use? And most importantly, how do you feel about those behaviors, styles, and methods?

I often teach what's traditionally called situational or adaptive leadership, which posits that we can and should change our leadership style based on the needs of our employees. In some cases, I as a leader might be very direct because the employee is new to a task and limited in experience and thus needs more guidance. In other cases, I might be much less directional and more empowering because I'm working with an experienced employee. Servant leadership, meanwhile, assumes that it's not about the leader; it's about the employee. The behaviors of the leader are designed to engage and empower the employee to be the decision-maker, the one who owns the project, and the one who advances the ideas.

Who we are is how we lead. Our assumptions play a big role in this dynamic, and if we don't understand them, we might behave in a way that causes a conflict. When I understand the assumptions at the root of my thinking, I can consciously choose whether or not to indulge them. I can even choose to ignore my assumptions. For example, if I assume that more structure is important for teamwork but am working with a gifted employee who performs better in a looser environment, I can choose to foster less structure. Understand how your leadership ideas have developed. What assumptions animate them? There might come a time when your leadership habits don't serve the situation. In such cases, understanding your assumptions will give you the flexibility needed to adjust accordingly.

Just as with determining our ideal life, we must be realistic when establishing our expectations about the ideal leader. Remain connected to yourself and your beliefs, not some pie-in-the-sky ideal. Being an authentic leader means talking and acting consistently to the best of your ability today. And then to try again tomorrow.

VITAL SIGN NO. 3
GROWTH MINDSET

Carol Dweck, the famed psychology professor from Stanford University, was first to introduce the difference between a growth mindset and a fixed mindset.[18] Someone with a growth mindset believes they can change and evolve through dedication and hard work. Someone with a fixed mindset, on the other hand, believes their abilities are innate and mostly unchangeable. In other words, you're either a born leader or not, a born communicator or not, a born public speaker or not.

Saying, "I can evolve or adapt," reflects a growth mindset.

Saying something like, "This is just who I am," reflects a fixed mindset.

When evaluating your mindset as a leader, it helps to locate yourself on the continuum between a growth and fixed mindset. Do you embrace challenges? Are you persistent in the face of setbacks? Do you foster a culture of learning and development within your team because you assume we can all learn and grow?

When assessing a leader's mindset, we can also use self-efficacy, or confidence, as a measurement.[19] Do you believe in your ability to accomplish goals and succeed in specific situations, or do you struggle to imagine your own success? I've known leaders in both camps. A leader that is vulnerable is willing to take risks and make mistakes. How do you balance being vulnerable with being self-confident? Many leaders fear that allowing themselves to be vulnerable will make them appear unconfident. But in fact, it takes a certain degree of self-confidence to reveal vulnerability. Would-be followers, of course, are looking for that certain degree of self-confidence but also respect a leader who is confident enough to admit when they do not know the best next step. And if you possess a growth mindset, then you know you can develop self-confidence over time.

I once worked with a young man who took on a management role in a very complex, high-turnover job. He started the job with zero management experience, and his self-confidence was low, but he spent time reading, thinking, and learning from more experienced leaders. During his first six months in the new position, he found himself confronted with some difficult situations: high turnover, legal challenges, harassment cases among his team members, fraud, and so forth. As he faced each challenge, he made a few mistakes, but he also made some wise judgments. Eventually, he built the kind of self-confidence that comes with leadership. Had he started out overconfident in his abilities, he might have made more mistakes—and burnt a few bridges along the way. Overconfidence can prove dangerous in a budding leader. Build your confidence as a leader by gathering feedback, seeking opinions, and reflecting on your successes and failures.

> Someone with a growth mindset believes they can change and evolve through dedication and hard work.

Along with a growth mindset and self-confidence, we can turn to cognitive flexibility when evaluating and building a leader's mindset. Cognitive flexibility—being able to adapt our thinking and our behavior in response to changing situations or new information—can help us keep up with the modern world's unprecedented pace of change. But adapting to technological advancements doesn't mean compromising our values or changing our principles on a daily basis. It merely means being prepared for and adapting to ongoing changes in technology, the process, and/or the status quo. Leaders who have been in leadership positions for a long time can struggle to adapt, largely because they believe they already know how to get things done—and often are confident that the old ways are the best ways. Leaders must be able to entertain new ideas and new perspectives. Nothing will disillusion employees, especially younger ones, quicker than refusing to hear their ideas. Leaders with cognitive flexibility can consider multiple perspectives, think creatively, and adjust their strategies as new resources and opportunities appear.

Let's take a moment to explore how we can develop a leader's mindset.

1. **Embrace challenges.** View each challenge as an opportunity, rather than a threat. Even the most difficult situation a leader can face hides one or more opportunities. As leaders, we have a responsibility to ourselves and to the people we work with to try to find opportunities, be curious, and be willing to learn.

2. **Learn from feedback.** A growth mindset requires us to be active listeners and embrace the feedback we receive, both positive and constructive. It requires us to reflect on that feedback and to be open to what we hear.

3. **Focus on learning.** As you were thinking about your ideal life, did you include how you plan to learn and continue to learn? It's an important part of what a leader does.

4. **Be accountable to the team.** If we act within a fixed mindset, it's difficult for our team to embrace a growth mindset. True accountability means modeling a growth mindset for everyone we lead.

Next, how can we enhance our self-confidence, whether we're new to the job or struggling to adapt to a rapidly changing world?

1. **Set achievable goals.** You can break goals, even loftier ones, into smaller subsets. It's in those smaller subsets that we start to build confidence in our abilities. We start to try things and stretch ourselves a little more. So begin with small steps.

2. **Seek mastery.** Take on the tasks that challenge you to keep stretching, and as you master those, your confidence will grow. Beginning with your natural strengths is an excellent place to begin to build mastery. Invest time and reflection in building upon your natural talent.

3. **Visualize success.** Although it might sound trite, begin with the end in mind.[20] Athletes have long relied on visualization as a part of their daily habits. As a physician leader, you can too. Surprisingly, research indicates that visualizing the outcome can produce many of the same performance improvement impacts as practice.

4. **Celebrate success.** This is a good rule not only for us but also for those we lead. Don't just move from one milepost to the next. Take a moment to celebrate how far you've come.

Finally, as we're cultivating cognitive flexibility, we can follow the following guidelines to better ensure our success:

1. **Practice perspective-taking.** This means having the ability to imagine walking a mile in another person's shoes. Think about the current situation from their perspective. What would be important to them? How would they see this specific situation? Cognitive flexibility encourages you to challenge your assumptions, to think a little broader than the way you might have thought in the past.

2. **Experiment with new ideas and new approaches.** When was the last time you tried something new? I have friends who have set a goal to do something new every year. They build vacations around it. They build entertainment around it. That

might be learning a new language, learning to code, learning to paint, or tackling a DIY project. Reading the *Harvard Business Review* or a popular leadership book or listening to a leadership-themed podcast are simple ways to expose yourself to new ideas and applications in leadership. Seek what you can learn from every activity, project, and/or social encounter.

3. **Practice mindfulness.** Meditation and reflection help us be more open to different mindsets, to recognize our own habits, and to challenge some of our own patterns.

As a leader investing in building a growth mindset, you can use self-confidence and cognitive flexibility to build not only your engagement but also the engagement of your team.

VITAL SIGN NO. 4
PERSONAL STRENGTHS

If I were to ask you to list your strengths and weaknesses, which would be the easier list for you to create? Most of us would point first to our weaknesses. In our society, from classrooms to boardrooms, we tend to emphasize addressing those areas in which we're weak. But I'd like to challenge us to first think about those areas where we're strong. What do we do well? How are we unique?

The Gallup organization and Dr. Donald Clifton, along with dozens of other researchers, have conducted decades of research on the concept of strengths-based leadership.[21] Each of us possesses a number of natural talents, and strengths-based leadership calls for us to focus on our strengths rather than our deficits. We should harness the power of learning to discover our unique strengths. To be clear, we're not talking about the tactical things that you can learn from an educational activity. How to make an incision, how to diagnose a specific disease state—these are things you learn and practice. What we're talking about here are those natural abilities that differentiate us from others—not *what* we do but *how* we do it.

The positive psychology movement and the strengths-based movement were founded on the concept that if we understand and utilize our strengths, we're more likely to be engaged in our work, enjoy it, and produce higher performance.

You've probably noticed that sometimes time flies by when you're working. When that happens, you might forget to have lunch because you're so engaged in what you're doing. You're in the flow. You've also probably noticed that sometimes time seems to stand still when you're working on a project. You don't enjoy the work. It's hard and feels tedious. Such moments—the flow state and the frustrated state—illustrate where you have natural ability and where you have less natural ability (notice I didn't use the word *weakness*).

The positive psychology movement and the strengths-based movement were founded on the concept that if we understand and utilize our strengths, we're more likely to be engaged in our work, enjoy it, and produce higher performance, and Gallup's research confirms as much. In fact, individuals that understand and employ their strengths every day are six times more likely to report having a great life.[22] If we understand and invest in our strengths rather than try to fix our weaknesses, we'll enjoy a greater return on our investment of time in performance yield. This is a hard concept for us to grasp because we have a tendency as a society and as individuals to focus on the negative and to talk about our weaknesses. In fact, many jobs describe their accountability as fixing failures rather than building excellence.

Siblings, although they come from the same DNA and are raised the same way, are often quite different in style and approach. I have three children, including two daughters, and my two daughters are both professional dance choreographers but attack their specialties very differently. My older daughter works out every step with discipline and precision before teaching the cast the first step. My younger daughter, in contrast, creates in the moment, allowing the mood and music to guide her as she works with the dancers. They each thrive as they leverage their individual approaches to create the integration of sound and movement.

A client of mine, a logistics manager, studied the logistical challenge of shipping materials from the US's East Coast to Japan via Europe and realized that he could save his company $2 million annually if he shipped them from the US mainland to Hawaii and then from Hawaii to Asia.

"Wow, this is amazing," I told him. "You've got this analytical capability that's such a strength for you."

He shook his head. "No, no, no. That's my weakness. People have told me my entire career I've got analysis paralysis."

It's true that any strength, when taken to its extreme, can be a detriment. But in this case, my client simply needed to learn how to manage his unique talent. You see, we each have natural talents, and these talents often become the lens through which we judge the value of the talents of others. His boss's talent was execution, and he therefore saw my client's natural talent of analysis as a frustrating impediment to his desire to execute. As a result, my client perceived that his talent was a weakness, but it saved the company $2 million! He and his boss came to an agreement that stipulated he would take two weeks maximum to study a problem before recommending a solution. He was the type of guy who would always say, "If I just had one more week, I could have created a better plan." But his boss convinced him that 98 percent of perfect was more than perfect enough. This was how he and his boss learned to employ his strengths for the betterment of himself and his company.

> Each of us faces the same challenge: to find where our natural abilities lie and to learn how to leverage them.

We like to pretend that all humans are created the same. In fact, some of us are much better at having a conversation with someone on an airplane or collecting and curating information than others are. Some of us are architects, creating and designing, while others are general contractors who bring that design to life. When studying the animal kingdom, we recognize the unique talents of some animals to climb trees, swim, or fly, and we don't expect them all to share the same natural capabilities. Similarly, we need to recognize that each human animal has a wide variety of talents that make us unique. Each of us faces the *same challenge*: to find where our natural abilities lie and to learn how to leverage them.

Plenty of treatments plans are available to a leader who's struggling to find their strengths, including strength-and-weakness assessments and psychological assessments. The Gallup organization's Clifton StrengthsFinder Assessment is one of many examples. A simple way to assess your strengths is to ask yourself the following questions: When am I at my best? Under which conditions will I best contribute?

In my case, you're going to get the best out of me when I have a chance to participate in the conversation and provide my ideas and perspectives. You're going to get the worst of me when I'm merely asked to execute something someone else has created. One of my strengths is finding different solutions and thinking about alternatives. Another way to find your strengths is to ask yourself and others: When do you feel like you're in a state of flow? What are the things you're doing when that happens? Don't look at just the skills you're exhibiting or the tasks you're performing; study how you're doing them. Remember: This isn't about the what; it's about the *how*.

> Knowledge of your strengths and the strengths of others enables you to build effective partnerships.

There are no cookie-cutter leaders. We all have our own motivations, strengths, skills, experiences—even our own crucibles (those challenging moments that have shaped us). Assessing those various elements helps you understand who you are. It helps you be a better, more informed leader whose actions are based on self-knowledge. I cannot overemphasize how important it is to identify your personal strengths. They are what make you unique. When executed they provide the energy and endurance to produce at your very best. This knowledge can help you in endless ways, including choosing a career, prioritizing possibilities, and defining your ideal life.

Let's spend a minute to consider the impact of your knowledge of your personal strengths on relationships. Truth be told, the reason we each have different strengths is for the common good. If we all had the same talents, daily life would not only be difficult (because someone needs to be good at doing our taxes), it would be quite boring. Some leaders think they must be the best at every task their team undertakes. After all, they are the leader, and leaders never ask anyone to do something they cannot do themselves, right? (More on this dangerous idea later.) The best leaders recognize the diverse talents of their team and leverage them for the common good to achieve the organization's mission. CEOs that believe they need to have all the knowledge required to run the company fail. Today's problems are just too complex. It takes a village to run an organization, and effective leaders know when to step up and when to let others execute. Knowledge of your strengths and the strengths of others enables you to build effective partnerships. Leaders who recognize when someone else has the best talent to execute the next task and give the space for them to excel are seen as participative and supportive. Leaders who believe they are the smartest, most talented person in every room quickly lose their influence.

Consider your current team. Can you identify two or three talents of each member? Can you identify which experience, perspective, or talent makes each member unique? When you're looking to fill a role, do you consider the talents that are needed to complement the team's current capability (both technical and nontechnical)? Effective leaders are tuned in to the capabilities and gaps of their team and plan work accordingly. Just as when you're engaged when you have the opportunity to do what you do best at work, the same is true for your employees. Consider creating a "strengths map" for your team. Engage your team in discussions about how they prefer to work and when they feel in their flow. This information helps the entire team know how best to leverage each other. Strengths-based leadership is a powerful way to build engagement and the performance of your team.

PREVENTIVE HEALTH ACTIONS (2-DO'S)
ACTIONS TO TAKE TO ENSURE HEART HEALTH.

Conduct a 360-degree assessment. Asking for feedback from your boss, employees, peers, and other stakeholders around you helps you learn how you're perceived by others, identify your potential blind spots, and discover your strengths. You can ask people to complete surveys online based on a set of competencies. Or you can simply ask them what you should start doing, what you should stop doing, and what you should continue doing. A 360 is best collected anonymously. That way, people feel they can be honest without damaging the relationship.

Invest in your sweet spot. Each of us has unique talents and unique interests. Where they intersect is your sweet spot. Seek to understand yours. What are the unique things that you bring to every situation? Your sweet spot will continue to motivate you throughout your career. Investing to continue to build your unique talents and strengths will return a greater ROI (return on investment) than trying to build skills in areas where you're not as unique or strong. You can find others who are strong to support you in those activities. Your strengths differentiate you from those around you, who will see you applying your strengths and passions and will follow suit. This is your superpower. Find it, hone it, and apply it.

For additional resources to support you on these vital signs, visit vitalsigns-book/resources.

As a physician leader, I don't just preach accountability. I live it. My colleagues need to see that I have skin in the game. I take service shifts, use the same technology that I expect others to adopt, and show up in the trenches. I know that accountability has to start with me. If I don't model fairness, transparency, and follow-through, I can't expect my team to do the same.

Whether I'm delivering a baby or solving an administrative problem, I make my commitments visible—like telling a patient, "I'll be back in five minutes to make a decision," and keeping that promise. In the same way when I make commitments to the team, I keep them. Even if I don't know the answer, I take an accountability to ensure one is found. That kind of consistency builds trust and holds me to the same standard I expect from others.

—Summary of interview with a physician leader: Chair, Woman's Health

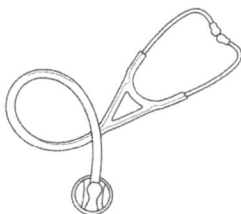

The A-ccountable Leader

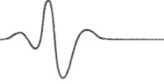

"You are not stuck where you are unless you decide to be."
—Wayne Dyer

PRESENTING SYMPTOMS ADDRESSED IN THIS CHAPTER

Missing personal goals.	Feeling like a victim.
Looking to pass the buck.	Overconfidence.
Others do not rely on you.	Feeling out of control.
Others complain to you.	Procrastination.

I n a busy urban hospital, Dr. Thompson was a senior physician renowned for his expertise and experience. Yet despite his impressive credentials, he had a troubling habit of neglecting the finer details of patient care, often dismissing small but critical tasks.

One afternoon, the hospital admitted Mrs. Green, a patient suffering from severe abdominal pain, and assigned Dr. Thompson to oversee her case. The initial diagnosis proved inconclusive, and Dr. Thompson decided to order a series of tests to determine the underlying cause. Dr. Thompson was known for his demanding schedule, often rushing from one case to the next. In his haste, he instructed his junior staff to proceed with the tests but neglected to review Mrs.

Green's complete medical history. The junior staff, eager to please and under pressure, didn't question the hurried approach.

A few days later, Mrs. Green's test results showed some alarming indicators that required immediate follow-up, but due to Dr. Thompson's oversight, no one reviewed or acted upon the results. The patient's condition deteriorated significantly. When a nurse finally raised concerns about Mrs. Green's worsening condition, she and others discovered that the critical test results had been overlooked. Dr. Thompson, upon learning of the issue, was quick to blame the junior staff for the oversight. He argued that they should have ensured that all critical results were flagged and brought to his attention.

As the situation became more urgent, another physician arrived to take over Mrs. Green's care. The new physician, after a thorough review, found that the delay in addressing the test results had led to severe complications that could have been prevented with timely intervention. The hospital conducted an internal review and found that Dr. Thompson's lack of personal accountability had significantly contributed to the lapse in care. While he had blamed others, his own failure to check the details and ensure proper follow-up had played a critical role in the mishap.

The hospital reprimanded Dr. Thompson and required him to undergo additional training in patient management and accountability. It also implemented new protocols to ensure that doctors promptly reviewed test results and clearly communicated responsibilities. The incident served as a stark reminder of the importance of personal accountability. For a leader of any organization, personal accountability is essential to success. In a health-care setting, it can mean the difference between life and death.

• • •

Accountability is a choice. It's a choice to own a task, to own your decisions, and to own the consequences of those decisions. So often we look for excuses for why things didn't work out instead of considering our individual accountability. Accountable leaders take ownership for their actions and their consequences in support of projects and their team.

> Accountability is a choice to rise above one's own circumstances and demonstrate the ownership necessary to achieve the desired results.

In the operating room, each individual—the surgeon, the scrub nurse, the anesthesiologist—has a specific accountability to deliver as the team works together to execute a flawless surgery. If someone shirks their accountability, it could be life-threatening. But elsewhere, whether in the boardroom or on the factory floor, we've all experienced being on teams where individuals didn't take personal accountability for the quality, timing, and consequences of their personal behaviors. As leaders, we need to look at our own accountability first.

We begin by making an honest assessment of ourselves and our choices and actions. And if one of our decisions leads to unfortunate consequences, we don't look for excuses. We don't blame the circumstances (e.g., a lack of resources) or point the finger at someone else (e.g., senior leadership) for their inattention to our needs. Personal accountability requires us to be honest about our mistakes. It requires integrity and a level of self-awareness that enables us to process our successes and failures. It's a difficult assignment.

In *The Oz Principle*, authors Roger Connors, Tom Smith, and Craig Hickman define accountability as a choice to rise above one's own circumstances and demonstrate the ownership necessary to achieve the desired results. Their definition makes two things clear: First, it's a personal choice; and second, it requires us to rise above our own circumstances.[23] If you're a surgeon performing a routine surgery that suddenly becomes more complicated, that doesn't give you an excuse to bail on the procedure or the patient. Similarly, a leader must remain accountable for a positive outcome even if a task or the circumstances around it change.

Accountability requires courage. Not only does it demand that we look at ourselves in the mirror and offer an honest assessment of our leadership; it means accepting that the buck stops with us as leaders; and it means summoning the courage needed to admit our mistakes, learn from them, and take action to rectify them.

Before we go any further, let's pause a moment to make a distinction between accountability and responsibility. Most dictionaries define the two words as synonyms, but I choose to differentiate accountability from responsibility while working with my clients. Grasping that difference will help you understand your unique role as a leader. While *both* accountability and responsibility require a personal choice and require us to rise above the circumstances, accepting accountability means taking ownership of our role in task accomplishment, while responsibility requires us to take ownership of not only our own action but also the actions of others. As leaders, we take responsibility for the actions and outcomes of the group even when others are accountable for execution. To be responsible means the buck stops with us. Even if others fail to take ownership of their tasks and fail to deliver, we still own the overall responsibility for a successful outcome. This is one of the great challenges of leadership. In order to successfully execute our responsibilities, we need the team members to be accountable for their roles in the execution. Leadership implies the act of assigning tasks to others and therefore assigning accountability to individuals and teams. Once assigned, we no longer hold these accountabilities to execute tasks, but that doesn't relieve us of our responsibility to ensure that the tasks are successfully accomplished. The completion of those tasks is the accountability of your team. As a leader, you're responsible for the final outcome.

Note the words: *final outcome*. Where leaders sometimes struggle, particularly when they're new to the role, is assuming they're personally accountable for every step along the way. This behavior is called micromanaging. Yes, part of leadership requires us to hold others accountable for their contribution to the process. But if we try to do others' jobs for them, we rob them of their personal accountability and reduce their ownership in the outcome.

A quick Google search of the word *micromanagement* brings up countless examples of managers or leaders not allowing employees to take personal ownership and accountability to execute a task on their own. Effective leaders recognize that as leaders, we're accountable for certain things like the development of our team. We're accountable to make sure we've built a safe work environment. But the individuals we lead must be held accountable for their own actions and outcomes.

By trying to be accountable for everything within the scope of our authority, we unwittingly train our employees to *avoid* accountability. My physician clients often complain about their teams not stepping up and being accountable, but in practice, they never *allow* the individuals to be accountable. The physician leader's job is to shape and manage expectations. Doing so makes it clear that the individual or team is accountable for both actions and outcomes and that the leader is responsible for team performance. A big part of leadership is learning to distinguish between your accountability and the various accountabilities of your team members. Failing to do so can lead to confusion—not only yours but your team's.

Plenty of tools are available online to help leaders articulate individual accountabilities across a process or project. For example, a RASCI (Responsible, Accountable, Supportive, Consulted, and Informed) assessment is a useful tool for outlining a project's workflow and identifying who's accountable for the execution of each step. But before you engage with any of these tools, let's check your vital signs as an accountable leader.

VITAL SIGN NO. 1
REFLECTIVE COURAGE

I have a friend who is among the best parents I know. Parenting, of course, is a specific example of leadership. What makes him different from most of us is that he has the courage to use himself as an example for his children—and not just as an example of good behavior but also as an example of bad outcomes. He's candid about the challenges associated with alcoholism, anger, and self-indulgence and their effects on himself and his family. He has the courage to admit his mistakes and is willing to risk that his children might look at him differently when they discover that he has made some dangerous and perhaps even stupid mistakes. His desire for his children to avoid those same pitfalls and to understand the consequences paid for those decisions outweigh his desire to be seen as the perfect father within a perfect family. His four children demonstrate a personal accountability that I truly respect, and I believe that accountability is in part based on their father's courage to tell the truth, no matter how personally uncomfortable it might be.

It takes courage to be self-aware, because self-awareness requires us to understand our strengths but also those areas where we're less strong, where others have greater ability than we do. It also takes courage to admit that we've made mistakes and will make more. Many of us aren't willing to admit our mistakes because we think it makes us look weak, like we're no better than anyone else. This unwillingness, coupled with a natural fear of failure, often prevents us from embracing accountability. If you're a leader who demonstrates a fear of failure, then you can expect your team to follow your example and demonstrate similar behaviors. If, on the other hand, you're like my friend who regularly acknowledges his mistakes in front of his children, you'll inspire honesty, vulnerability, and personal accountability.

Fear of failure is closely related to imposter syndrome: the fear that we really aren't as good as everyone thinks we are; that we are, in fact, hiding significant flaws and shortcomings. If you suffer from imposter syndrome, it's likely that you'll try to hide, rather than expose your vulnerability. Such a lack of self-esteem is deeply ingrained and often learned at a young age from parents, teachers, and coaches, only to be reinforced later by bosses and even peers. It causes you to fear taking action.

This is why it takes courage to lead, and courage to want to serve as an example for other people. It takes courage to say, "I'm not comfortable, but I recognize that part of my accountability is to step up and take a risk, to move an idea or process forward, even when I'm not 100 percent confident in myself or the idea."

The answer isn't to become prideful or headstrong. We need only to be honest with ourselves about our strengths and those areas where we still need to grow. Honest self-assessment makes wise action possible.

How can we treat a lack of courage and invest in strengthening our self-esteem? Here are a few best practices:

1. **Reflect regularly.** Set aside time on a regular basis to reflect, whether that means thinking alone in your office, journaling in a notebook or on your laptop, or talking with a trusted adviser. A courageous leader recognizes their strengths and underdeveloped skills and learns to take accountability for the former while allocating to others (whose strengths complement their own) the accountability for the latter.

   As part of your reflection, try rehearsing ideas, discussions, and delivery of content to other people before it happens. Consider a few alternatives that can be pursued. After a big project or initiative, get together with your team to debrief. When I was in the nuclear industry, we were required to debrief after every project. What worked well? What didn't? What could have been done better? How could we have leveraged our strengths and resources better? What got in the way? How did we address that? How could we have addressed barriers in different ways? What did we learn for the future?

An important part of reflection is not beating yourself up about what you did or didn't do, but rather, moving forward in a way that enables you to understand how to better deal with similar situations in the future.

2. **Be like a goldfish.** After his soccer team delivers a particularly poor performance, sitcom character Ted Lasso asks his players, "What animal has the shortest memory?" To which the team answers, "A goldfish." When you've learned what you can from a supposed failure or letdown, be a goldfish. Move forward and forget it.

   And be like Simba in *The Lion King*. When Rafiki, the wise old mandrill, hits him over the head with a stick, Simba asks the obvious question: "What was *that* for?" Rafiki, who's trying to teach Simba how to move beyond the past, answers, "It doesn't matter. It's in the past." You can either run from the past or learn from it. When Rafiki takes another swing, Simba ducks just in time, having learned his lesson.

3. **Seek feedback.** Be open to the feedback of others. Take the risk of asking people how well you and your team performed. That's a risky, courageous question, because they might come back and say, "Amazing!" Or they might also come back and say, "Well, you underdelivered or failed to meet expectations." Seeking feedback builds accountability—not only for the behaviors we seek but for the outcomes we want produced as well. As a leader, you can also ask for feedback regarding your

responsibilities. What could you have done better to enable the individual or team to own their project, actions, and/or outcomes? How did you enable their success or hinder their progress?

Remember not to shoot the messenger. Even if someone gives you feedback that's difficult to hear, thank them for their input and then process the information they've shared.

4. **Start with positive affirmations.** Recognize your strengths and your positive contributions to a project or a task. Some of us are very good at this. We're quick to see how we contributed positively. But others can struggle a bit and are much better at articulating where they've failed. Acknowledging our strengths and successes takes practice.

5. **Adopt small goals.** If an individual or team is struggling with self-confidence, start with small steps to build their confidence. Just like Olympic gymnasts start with small steps to build to the ultimate routine, leaders and their teams must build confidence in themselves to be able to take those steps each day.

6. **Find a coach.** If you struggle with self-esteem or imposter syndrome, engage a coach. A coach, therapist, or counselor can help you with the neuropsychology of reprogramming your brain to think differently about situations, to build more confidence, to build more self-esteem. It takes courage to get help. Your limitations, particularly as they relate to accountability and responsibility, are going to directly impact the productivity of your team, because they're going to directly impact *your* ability to influence and lead them.

A leader's courage is a defining characteristic.

VITAL SIGN NO. 2
VICTIM MINDSET

Have you ever noticed how, when something goes wrong, instead of holding ourselves accountable for the results and trying to find a positive way out, we tend to spend our energy and effort trying to assign blame to other people? We call this the blame game. When we play the blame game, we say, "Well, it wasn't me. Someone or something else caused this." As soon as we say that, we're not holding ourselves accountable, because we're not taking ownership; we're pushing it elsewhere.

Sometimes circumstances *do* cause an outcome to go south. Nevertheless, the accountable leader takes ownership of the difficult situation they're facing in order to find a solution or a path forward. Can you see how the blame game expends a lot of time and energy looking backward? We should look backward just long enough to learn from our mistakes and successes. To assign blame, to point fingers, is a natural human reaction, but it's not the reaction of an accountable individual. An accountable individual recognizes the situation, takes ownership of actions taken and decisions made, and then moves forward to find better solutions. It's forward-thinking.

In *The Oz Principle*, Connors, Smith, and Hickman use a practical term to describe the actions involved in the blame game: "below-the-line behaviors." Sometimes in our conversations, particularly as we're working to finish a project or evaluating barriers preventing us from doing so, we fall below the line. We blame others, point fingers, deny that there's a problem.

We can also fall below the line in a more passive way: We just wait to see what happens. In such cases, we're not actively engaged in problem-solving or moving forward. Or perhaps we just ignore the issue and hope it goes away. Or we say, "That's not my job" (i.e., "It's not my job to make sure that every customer we work with is happy; my job is to deliver the product."). Others check out and give accountability to someone else. They say, "Just tell me what to do." This way, they don't have to take personal responsibility for their actions and outcomes.

The blame game is similar to the victim mindset. Have you ever heard yourself describing the results of a project or outcome by talking about why it didn't work, about the situational constraints, about how you didn't have enough control over the environment or the situation, about how the resources were too meager or the timeline too short? When we blame the circumstances or other people, our focus isn't on what's possible; it's on what's *not* possible. Instead of exploring a problem-solving idea, we focus on our limitations and why we *can't* do something.

After performing a procedure, particularly if that procedure was less successful than desired, surgeons often conduct M&M (morbidity and mortality) meetings, or clinical reviews. The objective in such a discussion is to understand the case, learn from it, and be courageous enough to identify any problematic details so that they can be corrected and/or avoided in the future. The purpose isn't to blame anyone or point fingers; it's to highlight the positives and move forward from what is considered a learning experience. Many physicians are quite adept at conducting M&M meetings, but too often when they talk about their own behavior as leaders, they're quick to blame others, to talk about the limitations of the situation, and to shrug off personal accountability. In other words, they assume the role of victim.

To be clear, some people really are victims—individuals who, through no fault of their own, find themselves in negative or dangerous situations. They have no choice. In contrast, most of us do

> The accountable leader takes ownership of the difficult situation they're facing in order to find a solution or a path forward.

indeed have choices. When we talk about a victim mindset, we're talking about those moments when we choose, consciously or unconsciously, to be a victim. Indeed, it's all too easy to slip into victim behavior. If you find yourself being defensive all the time, avoiding certain circumstances, or complaining about unfair treatment or unfair situations or consequences, it's likely you're indulging in a victim mindset. On the other hand, if, despite everything, you're determined to rise above your circumstances and supposed limitations, you're taking accountability.

> If we wish to be accountable to ourselves and our organization, we must leave behind finger-pointing and the blame game and move forward as quickly as possible toward positive solutions.

As a leader, if you demonstrate a victim mindset, an interesting phenomenon will likely unfold: Your employees and team members will begin to come to you with their problems, issues, and concerns to explain how they are also victims of their circumstances. Those with a victim mindset will find in you a sympathetic ear—someone they hope will accept their lack of accountability and reinforce their self-limiting beliefs.

When your organization engages in a cost-cutting initiative that has a direct impact on your department, how do you react? Do you address it as a victim? "Oh, this is so terrible. They're treating us unfairly. They don't understand our situation." Or do you take proactive measures to make the best of the situation? For many of us, the victim mindset is difficult to transcend. When we become angry with someone, we tend to say things like, "You made me mad." In fact, we decided, perhaps unconsciously, to react with anger to someone else's behavior. In such cases, the other person's behavior is an antecedent; we get to decide how to behave in response. This is a hard concept for someone with a victim mindset to accept because they believe that their life has been driven by circumstances, by those things around them, most of which they claim are out of their control.

Successful individuals, particularly those who have risen above difficult situations, share a common characteristic: resilience. We'll talk about resilience in more depth later. For now, we can understand resilience as the antidote to the victim mindset. It takes resilience to accept difficult circumstances and focus on moving forward as best we can.

It's not uncommon to fall below the line. But if we wish to be accountable to ourselves and our organization, we must leave behind finger-pointing and the blame game and move forward as quickly as possible toward positive solutions. We must decide to own our own actions and the consequences thereof. Whether we're leaders, influencers, or parents, we need to help those around us take owner-ship of their own behavior, and that starts with leading by example.

How can we treat a victim mindset?

1. **Listen to the language you use and acknowledge and accept that sometimes you operate from a victim mindset.** Acceptance often constitutes the first step in moving forward. When I'm dealing with clients who find themselves in a victim mindset, they often struggle with this first step. But we can't move beyond a victim mindset before first acknowledging it. By listening to our own words, explanations, and excuses, we can recognize when we play the victim. Great leaders choose to move beyond the victim mindset toward personal account-ability—even when it's hard.

2. **Identify and challenge those beliefs that might be limiting you and contributing to a victim mindset.** All too often, we operate from beliefs that limit us. When we examine those beliefs and recognize how much they're holding us back, we

can move beyond them. Limiting behaviors are those personal beliefs or practices that get in the way of our success. They're often based on historical experiences or the perceptions of those experiences and what led to failure. "I'm not good enough." "I don't deserve success." "I must be perfect to succeed." "I'm not smart enough." These are all beliefs about ourselves that limit our opportunity and energy for success. Limiting beliefs about the situation can thwart our achievement as well. "Success is only for a select few." "I have no control over the circumstances." "I don't have the resources I need to succeed." "There's not enough time." It can be difficult to recognize these limiting beliefs in ourselves and even harder to address them. We often perceive limiting beliefs as factual. To that end, I recommend leaders build the skill of being a contrarian so we can challenge the assumptions we make about ourselves, situations, and our team in order to open ourselves to new options and new possibilities.

> Real leaders focus on finding solutions, not making excuses.

Remember: Even when the proverbial deck seems stacked against you, you get to decide how you will respond. The behaviors of others do not "cause" our reactions. We decide on and are accountable for our reactions to their actions. We actually get to choose how we will react to almost every situation—even those that seem beyond our control. Separating fact (details) from fiction (assumptions and limiting beliefs about self, others, or the situation) isn't easy and can be emotionally charged, but accountable leaders challenge themselves and others to think critically, not just emotionally.

3. **Reframe your perspective and adopt a growth mindset.**
Remind yourself that you're doing the best you can. You're

moving forward. So you can cut yourself a little slack. Be like Ted Lasso's goldfish and leave your past mistakes behind. Their only value at this point is instructional. Practice some self-care in this context and make time for reflection, recreation, and exercise. Explore a relaxation or mindfulness technique to help keep you in balance and move you out of a victim mindset. And don't be afraid to reach out for support from a coach, mentor, or someone in your network who can help you move forward.

The victim mindset is easy to recognize in our politicians, who always seem eager to blame others or circumstances for their behavior or resulting undesired outcomes. Real leaders focus on finding solutions, not making excuses.

VITAL SIGN NO. 3
OUTCOME OWNERSHIP

When we take ownership of something, the feeling is almost magical. Think about that first car you bought. Maybe it required some maintenance. Maybe it wasn't the most beautiful thing you'd ever laid eyes on. And maybe you had to take out a loan to buy it. But once you drove it off the lot and it became yours, you felt a commitment to it unlike anything you'd ever experienced.

As a leader determined to take personal accountability, you experience a similar phenomenon when, for the first time, you take ownership of a project or a team. The operations, the outcomes, the consequences—all belong to you now—and that giddy-yet-sobering feeling inside connects you to something larger than you: your team, your department, your organization. Your world has grown.

Much can get in the way of our willingness to take ownership. Sometimes we feel like other people want to own the same thing, and conflict ensues. Other times, we're not sure what the expectations are of us and, therefore, if we should we claim ownership. It's hard to step up and be accountable for something when you're not sure what that ownership means precisely. Maybe there exists a lack of resources or a lack of support, which can influence our willingness to take personal ownership. Being willing to take ownership of something means understanding the parameters involved and weighing the pros and cons of making such a commitment.

If we go back to that first car, the decision felt more real once you signed on the proverbial dotted line and committed your financial resources to making it happen. At that moment, you became invested. That investment was *ownership*. The same is true for every leader, who must think about how invested they are in a project and the results. That distinction—between the project and the results—is worth noting because sometimes we can be invested in an activity and forget that our ultimate goal is not the activity but the desired outcome. So, we can spend a lot of time modifying that first car to make it look great, but unless we're able to drive it from point A to point B, we fall short of our ultimate goal.

Sometimes to ensure results, we must go above and beyond what we anticipated initially. We buy that car and discover that the radiator is leaking or that the tires need to be replaced. Because we own it, we're willing to make that extra investment. We want a car we can commute to work in and use for the occasional road trip. We're willing to invest in new parts to make sure that happens, and we continue to set money aside for oil changes and regular servicing to make sure our car is reliable and fully able to deliver the results we want.

> The clearer we can be about the tasks and outcomes, the easier it is to be accountable.

Similarly, when we take ownership as leaders, we feel inspired to go above and beyond. We invest our time and energy into team leadership and team membership, which is critical not just for us as leaders but also for every member of the team.

What is the treatment for a lack of ownership?

1. **Connect to your values.** If the result is important enough to us and is connected to our values, then we're willing to give the kind of time required. A clinical examination of a patient might only be scheduled for fifteen minutes, but sometimes you have to invest more time, energy, and resources than what you anticipated because you're so committed to your patient's health, and to the outcome that you're trying to achieve with them.

2. **Clearly define the scope of your accountability.** If you understand how you and others contribute to a project, if you're clear on where your accountability starts and where it ends

and where someone else's starts and ends and what those overlaps might look like, then it's easier to take ownership. As a leader, sometimes you define accountability for yourself and the team members in terms of specific roles (e.g., product design, sales, marketing, service delivery) sometimes defined by a job description. Other times the accountabilities are more vague and may overlap with other team members (e.g., find potential clients, ensure customer retention). The clearer we can be about the tasks and outcomes, the easier it is to be accountable.

3. **Define your requirements.** Articulate what you need in order to agree to take ownership of and accountability for the outcome. There is value in articulating up front what you need in order to feel comfortable taking accountability. No one ever wants to step up to something if they feel they can't be successful, but the accountable individual takes the next step to define the criteria under which they can take ownership.

Taking ownership as a leader is the first step in helping the team take ownership of the defined team mission and deliverables. When a team has a commitment to the desired outcome and shares in the rewards associated with success, team members begin to view themselves as owners. Everyone, no matter their position or individual role in the team or process, can view themselves as an owner. When employees feel like owners in the business, they're more likely to demonstrate personal accountability for execution. Successful leaders build opportunities for employee ownership in process execution, product quality, and service delivery.

VITAL SIGN NO. 4
RELIABLE EXECUTION

To be seen as accountable, you must also be reliable, and your reputation for reliability is based on people's perceptions and observations of your behavior. You might be highly talented and acclaimed, but if you don't practice wise time management, if you put off tasks and responsibilities, if you avoid addressing conflicts or difficult situations, if you overpromise without delivering results, your team eventually will recognize that you're unreliable.

Because of the nature and importance of their work, physicians are well regarded in society—and rightly so. Most are highly educated professionals and quite talented in their field. The challenge for many, however, is to retain a certain degree of humility, which is required to effectively lead. If you're a surgeon, for example, you

> As an accountable leader, you're required to focus less on receiving deference and more on achieving your organization's desired outcomes.

might be the most educated person in the operating room, where you have direct control over everything. But when you leave the OR, you might rely so heavily on your expertise that you forget the softer elements associated with leadership. Because you're such a critical part of the surgical team, you could easily find yourself considering your time and opinion more important than anyone else's. You spent years training, after all, and you perform lifesaving surgery every day, so you deserve a certain level of respect. As an accountable leader, however, you're required to focus less on receiving deference and more on achieving your organization's desired outcomes.

A typical challenge for many physician leaders is that, often while working so hard to take ownership of the big things, they forget the little things, and their fellow employees judge their value as a leader—not as a physician—based on those little things. For example, if your time management skills lead you to always being late for meetings, some people might let that slide, given your role as a physician. After all, you often must deal with emergencies and complications that take priority. But when *everything* becomes an emergency, when you're consistently late for meetings or manage your time poorly, whether due to procrastination or a lack of self-discipline, your team will judge you. Again, they'll probably still value you as a top-notch surgeon or clinical researcher, but they may come to view your leadership in a negative light.

> A great leader can be relied upon to be a source of help but not always a source of solutions.

As you think about how to bolster your reliability, I would encourage you, first of all, to never overcommit. It's easy for those of us aiming at big goals and trying to meet the expectations of those around us to overcommit, but when we overcommit and then miss timelines or deliverables (or find ourselves shortcutting processes), people notice, and it affects how they view us as leaders.

Some argue that our perceptions of leaders are built during times of crisis, because in times of crisis, some people prove extremely reliable. We can count on them to communicate regularly. They help us understand problems, finish projects, and weather difficult crises. Other people become victims during a crisis. Even *leaders* become victims, pointing at upper management ("They're not meeting their responsibilities!") or complaining around the water cooler ("That department is behind schedule!"). You can't be accountable in a crisis if people can't count on you.

Some people suggest estimating what 75 percent would look like and committing only to that, knowing that your real goal is to over-deliver (100 percent), which will demonstrate your reliability to others. Regardless, when you recognize the scope of your responsibility and accept your individual accountability as a leader, you're more likely to prove reliable. Your responsibilities might change over time, but your accountability to be a reliable leader, to be someone your team can count on, remains the same.

Be careful not to take on what I like to call "other people's monkeys." A vintage training program video, long since lost to time, talked about how people often try to get the monkey off their back and put it on someone else's. They come to you, their leader, with a problem, and rather than help them solve the problem, you take accountability for it. Here again, we must distinguish between responsibility and accountability. Your responsibility is to help that person solve their problem, not solve the problem for them. If I take on everybody's problems/monkeys, I take them off their back and put them on mine, and then it becomes nearly impossible for me to be reliable because I'm trying to manage too much.

It's preferable to demonstrate that I can be relied upon to help people solve their problems without taking their problems on myself. I can't teach my team how to be accountable if I keep taking away their accountability. A great leader can be relied upon to be a source of help but not always a source of solutions. Understand your scope of accountability and work to deliver that very specific scope.

Let's return a moment to the subject of meeting management. Have you ever noticed that most meetings are one hour long? Some are shorter, and some run longer, but most clock in at about an hour—even if far less time is required to discuss what needs discussing. If it only takes twenty minutes to solve a problem but we take sixty minutes to discuss it, we're creating an expectation that every problem takes sixty minutes to solve. Some of them might take twice that long to address, and some might require only a few minutes. As you assess how you manage meetings, ask yourself the following questions: Are you reliable? Do you start on time? Do you end on time? Do you expect everyone else to start and end on time? Can others rely on you to come to meetings prepared? Do you hold other people accountable to come to meetings prepared? Notice how those things influence how people perceive your reliability. If you commit to behaving reliably, your colleagues will learn to count on you and will be able to plan and execute their tasks more effectively as a result.

> If we have a proactive mindset, we're ready to attack a problem rather than waiting for a problem to come and attack us.

Finally, take a moment to consider the relationship between consistency and reliability. If we encourage employees to learn from their mistakes, for example, but then start punishing them when they make mistakes, we're sending an inconsistent message to our team. "Am I supposed to rely on you and trust you to allow me to learn from my mistakes," the average team member might ask, "or are you going to punish me for my mistakes?" If we lead in a consistent, coherent manner, no one on our team will have to ask such questions, and they can count on us to demonstrate our reliability.

As leaders, can we be relied upon to be proactive versus reactive in how we lead? Being accountable is not a wait-and-see activity. To be accountable, we must be proactive, not just reactive. For physicians, responding quickly to presenting problems, like a patient with appendicitis, is part of the job. Physicians also understand that proactive measures can be taken to support good health (e.g., regular exercise, getting plenty of rest, eating whole foods, reducing stress, and so forth).

Similarly, physician leaders must be reactionary *and* proactive to ensure good team health. Now sometimes it's appropriate to show patience and to allow the big picture to develop, but what I'm talking about here is a mindset. If we have a proactive mindset, we're ready to attack a problem rather than waiting for a problem to come and attack us. Part of the accountability of a leader is to anticipate potential roadblocks and brewing storms and to recognize opportunities before it's too late. We'll talk more about developing foresight later in the book, but for now, let's consider our current propensity for proactivity. Would your team describe you as proactive or reactive?

Here are a few tips to train your mind to be more proactive:

1. **Set clear goals.** Planning ahead, by its very nature, is a proactive activity. You're recognizing what needs to happen, and you're shaping a plan to make it happen.
2. **Identify priorities.** You can't do everything at once. Focus on your top priorities and plan accordingly.
3. **Anticipate challenges.** A well-conceived plan considers potential complications and problems. It also considers alternatives toward resolution ahead of time. This way you can take immediate action when crises arise.

As we become more proactive, it's easy to feel overwhelmed by everything that needs to be done. If we're not careful, it can feel like we have too much on our plate. The answer is to prioritize. Make a list of potential projects and outcomes for the next fiscal year, and after discussing all the possibilities, pick three to pursue. Our CEO at Respironics instructed our senior leaders to do exactly that at a meeting one day. The exercise taught us that everything can seem like a priority, but when everything is a priority, *nothing* is a priority. If we lack focus, there's no end to the number of projects and outcomes we can chase, no end to the demands that demand our attention. On the other hand, if we zoom in on a specific goal and what needs to be implemented to reach that goal, we can move forward with confidence. Identifying and pursuing priorities is an inherently proactive activity. It's essential to planning, and once we have a plan in place, we can focus on completing individual tasks.

A proactive approach sometimes requires us to build new relationships, whether with various team leaders, someone from another department, or outside experts, to achieve the goals for which we're accountable. Ask yourself the following questions: What's going to help me grow personally? What's going to help my team advance? Who needs to be involved? Who can help us? The answers will point you in the right direction, and if you're proactive, if you're ready to own the outcome, you'll make new relationships as needed.

Maintaining a positive attitude is critical to nurturing proactivity. It's not necessary to become a Pollyanna or ignore constraints. In fact, recognizing and anticipating constraints should be part of any proactive approach. Likewise, we can be proactive in celebrating successes and recognizing people's accomplishments, including our own. Let's start there and give ourselves credit for the things we've accomplished. We're often taught not to reward ourselves because it sounds egotistical, but we all benefit from self-talk and self-encouragement. Once you've accomplished a difficult task, celebrate your success. Reward yourself with a leisure activity, take time to enjoy a specific hobby, or get together with a friend you enjoy being around but don't see nearly enough. Do something proactive for yourself, and do something for your team—the kind of thing that will endear you to them.

PREVENTIVE HEALTH ACTIONS (2-DO'S)
ACTIONS TO TAKE TO ENSURE HEART HEALTH.

Commit to staying above the line. When we adopt the victim mind-set, focusing on the negative or placing blame rather than finding solutions, we fall below the line. As leaders, we must challenge ourselves to stay above that line. Listen to yourself. Watch yourself. Notice when you're falling below the line, acknowledge it, and move above it. When we stay above the line, we encourage our employees to do the same, both by our example and our direction. If we don't stay above the line, neither our example nor our direction to others will ring true.

Reflect on success and failure. Growing as an individual leader takes time and self-reflection. Why were we successful? Why weren't we? How could we have done that differently? What can we learn from that situation and from our emotions? And how can we apply that to better lead in the future? To improve as leaders, we must reflect on our leadership journey, from past to present. Did I act in an accountable manner? Did I play the victim? How can I take greater ownership of my work? How can I help others do the same?

For additional resources to support you on these vital signs, visit
<u>vitalsigns-book/resources</u>.

As a physician leader, I've learned that resilience isn't about being unshakable. It's about being adaptable, open to learning, and steady in your values. When I model that openness—whether it's reframing a challenge or soliciting a better idea from the team—it helps everyone stay grounded. I remind myself that I'm not just solving clinical problems anymore. I'm navigating people, systems, and change. That takes intention and reflection.

Resilience begins with self-awareness. I need to understand how I'm wired—what fuels me, what drains me, and how I recover when things don't go as planned. I've learned that leading today isn't about perfection or control; it's about being humble enough to fail, adjust, and keep going. When expectations go unmet, I don't deny the disappointment. I acknowledge it and then work to restore my energy and perspective.

I make time for activities that restore me, like hiking in nature, and I regularly reflect on what I need to stay grounded. Without that foundation, I know I won't lead effectively through the ambiguity that defines health care today.

—Summary of interview with a physician leader: Chief, Psychiatry

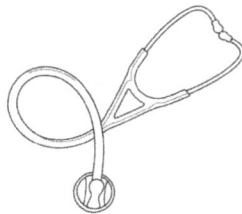

The R-esilient Leader

"Enthusiasm is common. Endurance is rare."
—Angela Duckworth[24]

PRESENTING SYMPTOMS ADDRESSED IN THIS CHAPTER

Exaggeration of consequences.	Making excuses.
Heightened tension.	Fear of failure.
Too critical of self.	Overwhelmed.
Hiding mistakes.	Burnout.

A leader must be able to excel not only during good times but during challenging ones as well, and to do so requires resiliency. Even positive change, the kind that comes with progress and an increase in responsibility, requires resiliency and the ability to adapt. The American Psychological Association defines resilience as follows:

> *The process and outcome of successfully adapting to difficult or challenging life experiences, especially through mental, emotional, and behavioral flexibility and adjustment to external and internal demands.*[25]

The English word *resilience* first appeared in the seventeenth century. Fittingly enough, it came from the Latin verb *resilire*, which means to rebound or recoil. When we call someone resilient, we're usually talking about their ability to bounce back from difficult situations. Indeed, leaders are typically judged by how they lead during difficult times and how they help an organization, team, and/or individuals bounce back and become more productive. I prefer to use the phrase *bounce forward* because it implies moving forward, not back, after facing a difficult challenge or disorienting change. Someone with resilience advances rather than retreats from difficulty.

"Don't judge me by my successes," Nelson Mandela famously said. "Judge me by how many times I fell down and got back up again."

> Someone with resilience advances rather than retreats from difficulty.

Resilience can't exist without accountability, which as we've already discussed, requires a willingness to rise above one's circumstances. Regardless of the difficulty, failure, conflict, or change we're facing, we have an opportunity—and the accountability—to bounce forward and grow. As leaders, we know we must enhance our individual resilience in order to build resilience in our team members and our organization as a whole.

Everyone experiences difficulties. Granted, some of us face trials that are much more dramatic than those of others. Some are physical, emotional, or spiritual. They form life's crucibles—to return to that term—that help define who we are. When asked, a leader will often tell you that the things that contributed most to their personal growth were the crucibles they faced, how they were resilient and bounced forward from those experiences.

"It's your reaction to adversity, not adversity itself that determines how your life's story will develop," says Dieter F. Uchtdorf, a German aviator and Mormon leader. In other words, we can't completely avoid adversity, but we can manage our reaction to it when it comes our way. Along with adversity, anything that challenges the status quo, anything that knocks us out of our routine or forces us to think differently, requires resilience, and fortunately, resilience is a skill, not an inborn trait, that we can learn and develop as we respond to change. It's often called a state-like trait. This means that although resilience is relatively stable, it can be developed, and it can be changed with experience, training, and coaching. We can learn and grow into it.

Early psychiatric studies on resilience focused on children from broken homes and impoverished areas, with researchers trying to determine why two children raised under the same circumstances fared differently. Of two siblings, for example, one might find a way to improve and escape the situation, while another might become stuck, never leaving their humble and difficult circumstances. Why? It came down to individual grit and determination. Those with resilience found a way to identify and define the situation, recognize its risk, and then find and follow a way out. They tended to be characterized by optimism and confidence in their ability to overcome any setback. They could learn from and adapt to conditions quickly and were willing to change what needed changing and to take risks to transcend their local situation.

An individual might call upon their resilience for any number of reasons, ranging from personal trauma to health problems or economic difficulties. Bouncing forward requires not only optimism but empathy toward oneself and others, with the latter often inspired by a moment in the past when someone else offered help during a difficult time.

While serving in Iraq in 2003, US Army infantryman J. R. Martinez was injured by a roadside bomb. Along with sustaining extensive burns to his face and body, he temporarily lost his ability to walk and returned home with post-traumatic stress disorder. Despite the physical and emotional challenges associated with enduring

numerous surgeries and extensive rehab, he showed immense determination and grit throughout his recovery and went on to become a
popular motivational speaker, using his experiences to inspire other
people. In 2011, he showcased his resilience and ability to thrive
when he won *Dancing with the Stars*.

Bouncing forward, turning life's crucibles into growing experiences, thriving despite our difficulties—all require resilience. Study
and monitor the following four vital signs to better understand your
own resilience and how you can lead yourself and your team to better
HEART health.

VITAL SIGN NO. 1
LEARNED HELPLESSNESS

Life is tough, and it's tougher for some than for others. Some might claim that the proverbial deck is stacked against them, but resilience is available to everyone. Failing to tap into it might prove more dramatic and more life-threatening for some than for others. Countless Americans require medical, legal, emotional, or physical support, and 3.5 percent of the US population wrestles with PTSD. Treatment often involves learning resilience behavior and thinking first of resilience as a decision. Indeed, like so many things related to leadership, resilience is a decision that individuals need to make for themselves. But the decision itself, although a critical first step, isn't always sufficient, because sometimes additional skills must be learned.

In 1873, German zoologist Karl Möbius conducted a study in which he inserted a glass divider into an aquarium and placed a pike fish on one side and several minnows on the other. The pike fish, known to be an aggressive predator, tried to attack the minnows as soon as it grew hungry, and each time it tried to prey on one, it slammed its face into the glass. Eventually, it learned to associate hunting the minnows with pain and gave up trying to feed on them. When the glass was removed, it continued to live passively among the minnows and would only accept food from its human captor. Pike Syndrome, as it has come to be known, describes a mindset of learned helplessness in which, even after circumstances change for the better, we fear risking failure and continue in our self-limiting ways.

Circus elephants used to be trained in similar fashion. Trainers would attach a band to a young elephant's leg and chain it to a huge tree, and the calf would learn that no matter how hard it pulled against the tree, it couldn't move. Eventually, the calf's trainers would remove the chain and then the band, but by then, even though the conditions had changed, the young elephant no longer tried to pull free.

Beginning in the 1960s, Martin Seligman and his research partners conducted pioneering studies on learned helplessness that showed how humans, much like an elephant calf or a pike fish, can grow so accustomed to pain or failure that we lose the will to succeed, even when conditions change. We see such examples in the workplace all the time. If, for example, your boss shoots down your ideas every time you offer them, you'll eventually learn that there's no advantage in taking such a risk, which is invariably punished.

Our task as leaders is to enable employees and team members to find the courage to try again—even if history suggests an unfavorable outcome. Yes, sometimes trying again can lead to disappointment and frustration, but if a single-parent sibling can find her way out of poverty and a broken home, we can summon the courage to tackle a challenge at work. Keep in mind that our single-parent sibling didn't just keep banging her head against the same glass; she adapted to her circumstances, trying different strategies and ideas in order to overcome her situation.

Do you suffer from learned helplessness? Do you find yourself saying, "Well, I have no control over the situation," "I'll do whatever someone else tells me what to do," "We've tried that before," or something similar? Such expressions are symptomatic of someone with learned helplessness. A new leader often finds themselves confronting the learned helplessness left behind by previous leadership. We have to find ways to challenge not only ourselves but those around us. How?

1. **Recognize the patterns that are connected to learned helplessness.** This is no easy task. People can entrench themselves so deeply in learned helplessness that they're not willing to hear that the glass divider is gone, that they're no longer tied to the big tree. Often, acknowledging our feelings of helplessness is the first step.

Next, we must remember that adversity isn't causing our problem; our reaction to it is. We can choose to try again. For some people, this is very painful and might require professional help in order to move beyond it. If you don't feel equipped to address something so overwhelming, seek help from a counselor, executive coach, or other professional. Always keep in mind that learned helplessness is a response to past experiences rather than a reflection of actual abilities.

2. **Maintain optimism.** Most setbacks in life are temporary, local (not universal), and often changeable. Paths to success are available to us—even if we've experienced years of frustration

> Our task as leaders is to enable employees and team members to find the courage to try again.

and learned helplessness. Committing to a positive attitude can help us change our beliefs about the situation.

3. **Start with small, achievable goals.** Break down tasks into smaller, manageable steps, and celebrate each step you complete. After all, every step, however small, takes us closer to our end goal. As we complete one step after another, we build confidence and a sense of control, which can counteract some of the helplessness that might be nagging us. Trying to tackle too big of a task can lead to frustration and anxiety, which in turn can reinforce helplessness. But a single failure doesn't necessarily mean that we will fail to complete the longer journey; it means only that we've failed in that attempt.

4. **Focus on what you can control.** Doing so helps reinforce our sense of agency and confidence. The Serenity Prayer can offer wisdom here: "God, grant me the serenity to accept the things

I cannot change, the courage to change the things I can, and the wisdom to know the difference."

5. **Develop some problem-solving skills.** If you practice problem identification—breaking down bigger issues into smaller components and addressing smaller problems—you'll likely feel more equipped to handle bigger challenges. There are dozens of problems-solving processes (e.g., plan, do, check, act) and tools (e.g., root-cause analysis, cause and effect diagrams, flowcharting) available to you to help you build problem-solving skills.

> As a leader, you can help others follow the path to resilience, but recognize that you can't make the decision to try again for anyone but yourself.

6. **Seek feedback and support others.** This can help reinforce and guide you in your journey toward resilience. Find other people who can support you along the way. People who've successfully gone through something similar are extremely helpful. Alcoholics Anonymous assigns everyone a sponsor/mentor who has gone through the same thing and who showed the determination and grit to move through it.

7. **Practice self-compassion.** Self-compassion helps you maintain motivation, recognizing that you are moving forward. Having determination and grit doesn't mean you succeed every time—setbacks are part of the process—but it means you get back up, as Mandela put it. Engage in positive activities that you enjoy and do well. Doing so can boost your overall self-esteem. Surround yourself with people that support, engage, and lift you up.

As a leader, you can help others follow the path to resilience, but recognize that you can't make the decision to try again for anyone but yourself. Not everyone has the same level of grit. Nevertheless, you can demonstrate it, discuss it, and build an environment that supports it.

VITAL SIGN NO. 2
MENTAL TOUGHNESS

To be resilient requires mental toughness. It requires us to have the strength to bounce forward in spite of the forces against us. Authors Karen Reivich and Andrew Shatté explore an important prerequisite to building mental strength: the ability to make the distinction between what they call AC thinking and ABC thinking.[26] When we engage in AC thinking, we begin with A, an action, and end with C, the consequence of that action. Most of us assume that the consequence (our response) is a direct result of the action we experienced or observed. We might say, "Your rude response caused me to fly of the handle." In doing so, we suggest that there exists a direct cause and effect response. In nature, this might be true. Step on a flower, and the flower dies. In human interaction, things are a bit more complicated than that.

ABC thinking, in contrast, inserts a translator between A and C: B. B, in this case, represents our beliefs about what we did or observed (action). These beliefs interpret our observations, and it's our interpretation (beliefs) that actually drives our reaction (consequences). How does such thinking play out in real life? Let's use a simple example. You suggest a new idea in a meeting, and your boss instantly shoots it down by listing concerns about your new idea. You start to feel the hair on the back of your neck stand on end, and your temperature and heart rate rise. Most of us would suggest that it was the boss's behavior that was driving your increase in anxiety and anger. A seemingly logical conclusion. But remember: Human interaction isn't that simple. If, instead, you were to slow down the A-C relational relationship enough to dissect the situation, you might ask what specifically is causing you to be upset. Is it the simple fact that your idea was challenged? Perhaps. More likely, it was the way your ideas were challenged and by whom they were challenged.

We often attribute motive and intent to the actions of others. We might make assumptions about why they acted as they did. "The boss doesn't respect me or my ideas." "They're threatened by me and want to see me fail." Both are examples of beliefs that might result in an anger response. What if these beliefs were wrong? In fact, what if the boss greatly respects us and believes that we're open and even invite challenges to our ideas? Would these different beliefs drive a different response in us? Perhaps acceptance rather than anger? We bring to any action assumptions about that action.

Thus, we can see that it's not the action itself that drives our response but our beliefs about that action: ABC. Our beliefs assign meaning (accurate or not) to the actions we experience.

> Our reactions (consequences) aren't inevitable.

Anyone trying to build resilience will recognize that AC thinking is a trap. It fails to consider how our beliefs determine our interpretation of events and thus the meaning of those events. How can we get an accurate read on the consequences of an action if our beliefs remain unexamined or are operating primarily on an unconscious level? If our kneejerk reaction to something is to feel anxiety or fear, we may experience any number of emotions: anger, sadness, depression, guilt, or embarrassment. How we react is based on our beliefs about the situation. Therefore, our reactions (consequences) aren't inevitable. We *decide* what we believe about the antecedent and respond accordingly. In one setting it might be anger; in another the same stimulus might cause guilt. The challenge is that this attribution of our beliefs is so quick we often do not realize the influence of the belief on our reaction. If we lose a big project we wanted to work on, we can choose to believe that we're being punished for something, or we can view it as an opportunity to direct our energy elsewhere.

Too often our reactions are all but programmed. Someone raises their voice, we get angry, and an argument ensues. But if we engage in ABC thinking, we slow down the process long enough to wonder about the person's motives. Are they really mad at us, or is something or someone else affecting their mood? By adding that step between A and C, we take charge of not only our beliefs but also the consequences we enact. When we engage in ABC thinking, no one in reality can push our buttons or force us to do anything—unless we allow them to, based on what we believe. True, we can't control the actions of others, but we can control the consequences we demonstrate in response to those actions. If I feel that my rights have been violated or that someone's trying to undermine me, that I've lost something of value or that I'm being viewed in a negative light, I'll react in anger or become despondent or embarrassed. And I'll likely draw a direct line between the person who has hurt me and my feelings about their actions. But when I take accountability for my beliefs, I suddenly realize that it's my beliefs about that action, not the action itself, that predict the consequences or outcomes. If I change my beliefs, then I can change my response or outcome.

Put another way, there's a difference between a passive reaction and a proactive response. The former is reflexive and seems beyond our control. The latter is deliberate and is a choice. Someone who habitually relies on AC thinking often feels triggered, like they have no choice but to feel the way they do. But a resilient person who uses ABC thinking knows they can find a way out of any problem and will view each dilemma as an opportunity to change and grow.

So what are some other common traps that ensnare our thinking?

- **Tunnel vision.** When we focus on the negative, we can't see what's right in front of us. A high-potential client of mine once shared with me their first performance review, which was praiseworthy with the exception of one statement: "There's opportunity for growth." Instead of acknowledging all the positives in the review, the client became fixated on that statement. "Opportunity for growth? What does that mean? Do they think I'm not doing the right things?" My client spiraled downward from there. Not surprisingly, tunnel vision can often lead to imposter syndrome.

- **Magnifying.** Someone who engages in magnifying makes everything into a catastrophe. But if every problem is urgent, *nothing* is urgent. If everything is catastrophic, *nothing* is catastrophic. Such thinking makes clarity impossible.

- **Minimizing.** The opposite of magnifying is minimizing. Maybe you've worked with that person who minimizes everything: "That's not important. Don't worry about it." Someone who minimizes everything is unable to realistically assess actions and consequences. We call such thinkers Teflon people: Everything slides off them because nothing is important or urgent.

- **All-or-nothing thinking.** This is sometimes called "the sucker's bet." I either have to be 100 percent correct, or I'm 100 percent wrong. Often, while considering alternatives, we find ourselves indulging the sucker's bet. The alternative is to recognize that a proposed idea or solution might contain both pros and cons. It's our job to accurately assess them and respond accordingly.

- **Personalizing.** When we engage in this thinking trap, we assume the world revolves around us. I've coached my share of executives who, regardless of the situation they face, focus on the impact someone or something is having on them. Such thinking demonstrates two extremes: Either everything is about me and everything is connected to me, or everything's my fault or my accountability. It's helpful in such instances to return to our distinction between accountability and responsibility. We might feel responsible for the outcome of a team project or organization-wide initiative, but we can't possibly be accountable for every task along the way.

- **Externalizing.** When we externalize something, we play the blame game. It's always someone else's fault. Personalizing and externalizing are similar in that each thinking trap is looking to place blame, either on myself or other people, rather than looking to understand and solve a problem by taking it apart and exploring the positive elements. Those who thrive and bounce forward don't waste time blaming someone or something; they look for solutions or resolutions.

- **Overgeneralizing.** When we overgeneralize, we say things like, "This always happens," or "This never happens." A lot of people that struggle with learned helplessness also engage in the overgeneralization trap. "My boss never listens to me." "My boss always treats me this way." We can help someone break out of that trap by helping them recognize that they're overgeneralizing every experience they have with their boss.

- **Mind reading.** I've said it a thousand times in my coaching career: You can't deal with people's motives; you can only deal with their behaviors. If we try to determine their motives, we start attributing things to them that might or might not be true. We start judging their every action and the motives behind them. Even a positive behavior, such as someone trying to support you, can be judged through the attributed-motives filter based on past history. We become suspicious. "They must be trying to set me up." The challenge here is to address directly the behavior and leave the attribution of motive behind. Sure, sometimes another's motives may appear to surface through their repeated actions, but to attribute motive to action is a risky game, and a game you can never win. It is too easy for others to deny the perception of attributed motive. Focus instead on the specific observable behavior without attribution of motive; then you can address the impact of the action directly. This simple advice saves relationships. Attributing motive is accusatory and often results in defensive behavior. Dealing with the observable behavior is tangible and allows direct resolution.

- **Emotional reasoning.** I'm not an advocate of separating emotions from decision-making, because that's not how humans make decisions. We can find valuable information in our emotions and in our emotional reasoning, but we must not allow emotions to dominate our thinking. Sometimes we can spot emotional thinking in the way we react to criticism. If we become angry or frustrated by someone's critique, it's often because we recognize some validity in it. We often know, if only unconsciously, that they've hit on something that we struggle with on a regular basis. Take the time to evaluate your thinking. How much of it is based on reflexive emotions? How much of it relies on sound logic?

- **Fear of Ambiguity.** Leadership often requires us to deal with unclear goals, directions, and expectations. We're often called to act even when conditions and consequences aren't clear. In fact, part of the job is to provide structure for our team when no structure exists. How we deal with ambiguity can become a thinking trap when we come to expect everything to be clear, defined, and evident. Rarely in today's world do decision-makers have access to all the data. Some of us use ambiguity as an excuse to delay or avoid our responsibility for action and/or results. Fear of ambiguity can paralyze some leaders. We can avoid this trap by taking accountability to actively seek clarity and direction. When required, we must act based on the best information available.

So how do we know when we're engaging in such thinking traps? More importantly, how can we avoid and/or escape them?

The first step is to recognize them wherever they occur in your thinking. This requires courage. Take a moment to ponder the traps above. Which ones apply to you? Maybe you're someone who tends to catastrophize everything, even small problems. Or maybe you're someone who jumps to conclusions or fixates on the negatives of every situation. Recognizing where your thinking has led you astray is 80 percent of the battle. Because once you recognize your thinking traps, you can choose how to act. If you don't recognize them, you'll act habitually in the same way you always have without understanding why you behave the way you do.

> Once you recognize your thinking traps, you can choose how to act.

To illustrate this point when I am teaching leadership classes, I instruct my students to cross their arms. Simple task, place one arm over the other. Then I ask them to uncross their arms and then cross their arms again. Most people return to their initial arm-crossing pattern. It's a habit. If you're used to crossing your right arm over your left arm, doing it the other way feels a little uncomfortable. In reality, you can choose which arm to put on top. You do not have to follow your habit. There's power in that. There's a choice in that. The application to our habitual thinking traps is the same. When we do not recognize our habits/behavior patterns, we most likely will repeat them. However, when we recognize our patterns of behavior, we can choose when to use them and when to violate them. The magic of recognizing our tendencies for certain thinking traps is that it allows you to decide how you want to act and not just fall into your habitual behavior. There's grit and thriving in that.

The Center for Creative Leadership encourages using a research-based, step-by-step approach to addressing thinking traps and negative beliefs. Doing so will help you build resilience.

1. **Accept change.** Remember that sometimes we find ourselves in thinking traps because we're reacting to a difficult situation or a change in our environment. The Center for Creative Leadership identifies this as the number one derailer of executives because they're unwilling to accept the reality of layoffs, salary adjustments, redesigns, and so on. They think they can deny change or postpone it.

   You must be willing to accept the reality of a situation. That doesn't mean you have to react in a certain way. Every action—even a difficult one—allows us to choose how we'll react. Understand and explore your beliefs and design the consequences/reactions that are most effective in helping you reach your higher-level goals. Accepting where we are grounds us and gives us a place to start.

2. **Build new skills.** Continuous learning is a trait of resilient people. It's also something we do when we recognize thinking traps and move beyond them.

3. **Empower yourself.** When we take control of our beliefs, particularly those operating beneath the surface, we take control of our own environment.

4. **Find a larger sense of purpose.** Recognizing our personal *why*, a la Simon Sinek, motivates us to bounce forward.[27] It increases our grit and determination.

5. **Claim your personal identity.** Who you are is not what you do. Recognize that you have value beyond your job/career/vocation/accomplishments. Allocating energy to self-discovery builds resiliency.

6. **Build networks.** Find those who have faced similar problems and draw from their experiences. Use benchmarking. Reach out to organizations that have gone through similar challenges or that are trying to implement similar ideas, policies, or procedures and vicariously learn from them.

7. **Reflect.** Encourage your team and members of your organization to think about the ABC of each situation they face. If they examine their beliefs, taking care to make sure they're not falling into any thinking traps, they'll make better decisions moving forward.

Let's take a moment to address a specific thinking trap that can paralyze us: fear of failure. How do we react to failure? It's part of life and an integral part of personal growth. Embracing failure can either turn into a downward spiral or motivate us toward an upward spiral. It offers valuable lessons and opportunities for development. As automaker Henry Ford once quipped, "Failure is simply the opportunity to begin again, this time more intelligently."

A close friend of mine worked for years in the outplacement business preparing people for layoffs. In this role, he saw firsthand how most people struggle to see losing their job as anything but a failure. In today's business landscape of "rightsizing" and other strategic moves, layoffs often say more about the company doing the firing than the employees being fired. But if you're one of those employees, it's awfully hard to see the big picture. When we tie our identity to job success, being laid off can feel like a professional and even personal attack. How can we not live in fear of failure after a catastrophic loss, poor decision, broken relationship or mistake? How can we reframe even a life-shaking event into a positive step forward?

Author Frank Vertosick Jr. references how neurosurgeons deal with failure.[28] Sometimes an individual makes a mistake, and sometimes conditions all but guarantee a failure. Neurosurgeons and other physicians have to figure out how to manage failure and grow from it. If someone dies on the operating table, how do we prevent something similar from happening again? How do we not allow it to destroy our confidence? A physician must learn to be accountable without taking failure personally, the latter of which can harm a person's self-image, self-worth, and future performance. The next patient deserves our very best, even in the face of a recent failure. Resilience is all about getting up after the fall.

Some of us set an impossibly high standard for our conduct, and when we don't execute every single element of a procedure or process flawlessly, we consider ourselves a failure. We forget that we're human, that sometimes we'll make poor decisions or react in haste. The challenge becomes this: How do we prevent failure from destroying our self-confidence and self-worth? How do we use it as a tool for growth? How do we bounce forward from even the most catastrophic outcome that resulted from a decision we made?

Sometimes physicians need to seek professional support to better understand failure. When I meet such clients, I remind them that if things nevertheless go sideways even after they follow the standard treatment protocol, it doesn't mean they failed. Failure isn't a yes-or-no matter. Performance is more nuanced. Yes, sometimes a physician might misdiagnose an illness or miss something, but just as often, complications arise that occur outside the realm of what can be predicted or controlled.

Because it's connected to our ego, failure in any form can be hard to accept. It can lead to uncertainty, anxiety, and even repeating the same mistake. Our negative emotions can delay our acceptance or recognition of failure, which prevents us from taking accountability and moving forward. Sometimes, failure leads to a perceived lack of control, which disempowers us. Other times, failure generates fear. We fear that people will judge us based on our failure, and self-criticism can make it difficult for us to confront even constructive feedback. It's true that sometimes people judge us for our failures, but they judge us more harshly when we don't *admit* failure, when we don't learn from failure, when we don't recognize our own vulnerability.

During the Olympic Games, while we celebrate the success of various athletes, we often neglect to notice that most of the people competing actually fail. Most don't make the finals or semifinals, much less medal. Even most of those who medal fall short of winning gold. How do those athletes cope with failing to meet the expectations of others and themselves? Do they feel shame for falling short?

> If we dwell on failure without transcending it, we can lose our ability to bounce forward.

When misunderstood or poorly processed, failure can lead to financial loss, damaged relationships, and missed opportunities. Worse still, fear of failure doesn't go away if we ignore it. It can lead to imposter syndrome. And if a high-producing individual fails once, they can feel shaken to their core. Ironically, failure is a real risk for high-producing individuals precisely because part of being high-producing means taking more risks, and as that risk level rises, the odds of not succeeding or meeting expectations grow.

Fear of failure can lead to stress and anxiety, low self-esteem, lagging confidence, the avoidance of new challenges, emotional burnout, negative relationships, stagnation in personal and professional growth, health problems, and even reduced resilience. If we dwell on failure without transcending it, we can lose our ability to bounce forward. Thus, our job as leaders is to help ourselves and others recognize, prepare for, and manage failure.

How can we do that? It starts by reframing how we view failure. Thomas Edison famously said of his efforts to invent the electric light bulb, "I have not failed. I've just found ten thousand ways that won't work." Daniel Boone, one of America's most famous frontiersman, quipped, "I have never been lost, but I was bewildered once for three days." Showing grit and determination means reinterpreting failure so that it elevates us. Imagine the difficult conversations that take place among physicians at morbidity and mortality (M&M) debriefings. Imagine sitting down with others to scrutinize a bad outcome involving you and your work. The critique and feedback will make you a better surgeon, a better physician, but it will be painful to hear, no doubt. We can make the experience more positive if we reframe it. To do so, we can practice the following techniques:

1. **Embrace self-compassion.** Be kind to yourself and recognize that everyone experiences failure. Show yourself the same understanding you would offer a friend. For some of us, that's extremely difficult because of our perfectionism. We can feel empathy for someone else, but it's hard for us to feel empathy for ourselves and our failures.

2. **Reflect and analyze.** Take apart your failure. Understand what went wrong, why, what you can do differently, how you can grow because of it, how you can adjust and make better-informed decisions in the future.

   In the nuclear power field, any failure in any system is studied and diagnosed, not to place blame, but to determine how to move forward. Encourage the people you lead to seek support from friends, mentors, and colleagues, all of whom can offer encouragement and help provide new viewpoints. A wise leader recognizes when they're struggling with failure and finds emotional and even professional support. That's not a failure. That's a critical judgment to get support. Eliciting the help of others shows courage and wisdom.

3. **Maintain a growth mindset.** Skills and abilities—resilience among them—can be developed. As you build out of failure, set realistic goals, and celebrate your subsequent successes. The Olympian who doesn't win gold often goes back to the basics, studies and hones their craft, and then elevates their performance to an even higher level. They bounce forward and learn to thrive. If you've got an admirable and important goal, let it motivate you toward further success.

Mental toughness is a critical characteristic of the healthy HEART of a leader. Ironically, building toughness requires us to express compassion and empathy for self and others. It requires us to confront our thinking traps and learn to positively frame failure. Our level of mental toughness and grit determine our capacity for resilience.

VITAL SIGN NO. 3
COPING SKILLS

Gillette ran a series of Dry Idea deodorant commercials in the 1980s that featured the tagline, "Never let them see you sweat." Implied in the antiperspirant ads was the notion that we shouldn't let people see our emotions or our emotional reactions, especially during high-stakes moments. As already mentioned, emotions play an important role in who we are and how we make decisions. That said, there's no arguing with the fact that as leaders, we're often judged largely on how well we fare during crises. Whether we're facing something like layoffs, missed targets, or divestiture, the spotlight will fall on our leadership. Any kind of change, even if brought on by outside circumstances like COVID-19, will act as a proving ground for our leadership. How well we perform will affect how others see us as leaders. Indeed, the ability to cope with expected *and* unexpected changes and crises is a hallmark of a great leader. How do you react in times of crisis or stress? What coping behaviors do you use to help you manage the impact of change to the status quo? How do you help your team positively cope with change in their daily routine?

> The ability to cope with expected and unexpected changes and crises is a hallmark of a great leader.

Elisabeth Kübler-Ross, the Swiss-American psychiatrist, is perhaps best known for developing a model for what she called the five stages of grief: denial, anger, bargaining, depression, and acceptance. Individuals, particularly those who have been given a terminal diagnosis or who have just lost someone close to them, tend to go through this common pattern in their grieving process. Only after they've arrived at the final stage of acceptance can they move forward. Unfortunately, many never reach it and remain lost in the grieving cycle. Each step in the grieving cycle must be made before reaching the final stage. Two actors, Christopher Reeve and Michael J. Fox, exemplify what it means to accept reality and move forward. Reeve, best known for his movie role as Superman, became a lifelong quadriplegic after an equestrian accident, but when reviewing the turn of events that put him in a wheelchair, he famously said he wouldn't change a thing. Falling off his horse had enabled him to become an effective disability activist. Fox, after being diagnosed with Parkinson's disease, battled depression and alcoholism before going on to start his own foundation and directing his energy toward advocacy.

Along with experiencing the five stages of grief, those of us coping with a big change or crisis can feel a sense of guilt for our inability to prevent the crisis. Confusion, too, can cloud our thoughts. The status quo has been destroyed. What do we do now? How do we do it? We can feel helpless, like something is being done *to* us. Stress levels almost always increase as we struggle to find a way forward.

As leaders, we must recognize how natural it is for people to grieve during a crisis or unprecedented change. We can show empathy and patience, allowing everyone to work through the various stages as they struggle to adapt to new software or a new patient-onboarding procedure. In a rapidly changing environment, as much as we'd like people to swiftly move from being productive in the old way to being productive in the new way, we must recognize that doing so takes time. An organization that doesn't allow its members to grieve the loss of the old way before growing into the new one can struggle to implement change successfully. We can also help people steer clear of negative or unhealthy coping behaviors, like alcohol or substance abuse, inappropriate anger or emotional outbursts, shooting the messenger, or playing the blame game (whether blaming ourselves or others). We'll be watched closely for our behavior during a crisis. If our team sees us ignoring or denying reality, various members will start questioning our leadership.

As author Jim Collins points out, often no one tells the senior leader about an impending crisis because they're afraid to harm the leader's vision of their creation or make them worry about failing to meet the board's expectations.[29] As leaders, we can be guilty of not only denying or ignoring reality but of pursuing unworkable or unrealistic solutions in response, all in an effort to preserve the status quo. But the organization suffers when its leadership is kept in the dark about a crisis or needed change. What follows are a few ideas to consider as you develop coping skills.

The first step in building effective coping behaviors is to put in place early detection. The best way to cope with a crisis is to prevent it. If we build expectations and infrastructure to look forward, then crises will surprise us less often. While I was at Respironics, a sleep medicine manufacturing business, we were determined to maintain market foresight, to anticipate changes so that we could lead rather than react to our competitors or new technologies that might intrude on our space. In the nuclear industry, measurement systems are put upstream to help people avoid crises. If we are diligent in near-miss reporting as part of our approach to safety, then we are more likely to avoid a catastrophic injury or event.

Next, as leaders, we must endeavor to manage our own emotional responses. Emotion can be an important tool for us, but if we regularly fly off the handle, we reduce our emotional influence. Our teams and employees recognize that we're out of control. This doesn't mean we have to be happy about difficult situations; it just means we need to be aware of the impact our behavior has on those we lead. If we act angry, we're not going to get the truth from our team, because they're going to be afraid of us and our reactions. We can use things like mindfulness, deep breathing, and relaxation techniques to help us stay calm. Something as simple as taking two or three deep breaths before we react emotionally allows us to regulate our emotions.

Cognitive restructuring, too, is available to us as we manage our coping behavior. Changing negative or unhelpful thought patterns to more positive and realistic ones can help us recognize the thinking traps explored earlier in this chapter. Start with your own thinking before addressing the thinking of others. The idea here is to search for the silver lining in every situation. Sometimes a crisis provides us with opportunities that wouldn't have been available otherwise.

> Coping skills are very personal. What works for one person might not feel natural to another. We each need to find those coping skills that work for us to help us depressurize the situation and our natural emotional reactions.

Thinking broadly about the situation involves looking for the root cause or causes, assessing how others might address similar challenges, recognizing the advantages of starting over, and identifying multiple paths forward with the objective to continue progress—to bounce forward.

Gathering data can offset our tendency to jump to conclusions. We really can't understand a problem, much less know which direction to take, until we have all the data available. And in those instances when we're forced to make decisions with incomplete data, we must be sure to study the data we *do* have and follow up with unbiased analysis. Similarly, we can apply problem-solving skills to help us cope with specific behaviors or problems. Brainstorming solutions, root-cause analysis, and other tools can help us address a crisis systematically.

On a personal level, we can seek social support to help us cope with the emotional and intellectual challenges we face. Friends, family, and others can provide not only emotional support but practical assistance as we grapple with our coping behaviors. They can provide ideas and alternatives to consider, but be careful. They can also drag you below the line and support your descent into victim behaviors. Find those individuals that can help you reframe and grow from the situation. Asking people for feedback on our coping behaviors can prove illuminating. As someone who struggles to maintain a poker face, I have to be careful about my facial reactions when presented with a challenging situation. Otherwise, people may misread them and interpret them incorrectly. Once, while struggling with my reading glasses during a workshop, I found myself repeatedly looking over my glasses at the students around the room. Afterward, someone in the class provided me with some critical feedback: They perceived that I had behaved condescendingly toward them as I stared over my glasses and looked down at them. Needless to say, their feedback inspired me to change my prescription.

How do you cope with change and crisis and build your own resilience? Do you practice relaxation techniques, meditation, or yoga? Author Shirzad Chamine references the tools that can be used to break the cycle of negative emotions, whether fear and anxiety or thinking traps.[30] He explains the power of using the physical to distract the mental. Simply rubbing your fingers together lightly can distract your brain and allow you to refocus your emotions. Alternately, taking a moment to count your toes, as strange as that may seem, can help you break free from a negative spiral.

When coaching leaders, I often suggest the use of positive self-talk. Think about how you would encourage other people to cope with change and crises. Then adopt that same talk for yourself. You can rehearse your positive self-talk while in an elevator or on a train or airplane; just be careful to think in your head and not out loud. Coping skills are very personal. What works for one person might not feel natural to another. We each need to find those coping skills that work for us to help us depressurize the situation and our natural emotional reactions. As leaders, we must provide an important example for our team: patience and the proper coping skills associated with resilience.

VITAL SIGN NO. 4
GRIT LEVEL

To diagnose your personal HEART health, consider your grit level. What is grit? It's the ability to persevere and stay passionate about long-term goals even when faced with outside obstacles. As its definition implies, grit contains two important elements: passion and perseverance. Passion relates to your personal *why*, to the thing that gets you out of bed every morning. When you feel passionate about something, it's much easier to find grit, because you have a deep interest in pursuing and sustaining your long-term goals. You're committed to them. Perseverance, meanwhile, enables us to continue working even in difficult times. When we recognize that something is worth doing and worth doing right, we wholly invest ourselves in it. Very few rewarding goals are accomplished in a short period of time. Most of them entail failures, setbacks, and delays. Persevering means remaining determined to move forward in spite of everything.

Grit provides you with the emotional energy needed to overcome challenges. It helps you push through difficult situations and remain steadfast, even when things might take longer than you thought they would or when they entail prolonged difficulties. Most of us can think of a moment when we overcame any number of obstacles because we were so focused on accomplishing our goal. Grit contributes to individual strength, courage, and power. It's an essential ingredient for anyone who wants to thrive, especially in times of crisis. Indeed, we want to do more than cope, don't we? We want to use crises to help us grow and adapt.

When we watch someone with grit, we notice how adaptable and flexible they are. They can adjust to new realities and find new ways to navigate old problems. They learn from experience as part of the adapting process. They show emotional strength, regulating their emotions and bouncing forward after moving swiftly through the recovery process. They embrace personal growth and a deeper sense of self-awareness.

Organizations exhibit grit by creating new strategies, ideas, and processes as a result of coping with a crisis. That's because grit motivates us and helps us build a positive outlook. It helps us gain confidence. When we survive something like a merger or a significant market realignment, we learn how to overcome the next crisis and craft a set of tools that can serve us in the future. More often than not, crises birth innovation and bring new opportunities. Creating a new way forward requires transformational change. Every crisis is, at its heart, a catalyst for significant positive change.

> Every crisis is, at its heart, a catalyst for significant positive change.

When we survive a crisis or drastic change, we can bounce back or bounce forward. Bouncing back means returning to the previous state of normalcy, function, and experience before the crisis. It means recovering from our difficulties and restoring the status quo. Sometimes that's an appropriate response: to be able to restore things to the way they were, to revert to past practices, particularly in the context of a short-term recovery. The great thing about bouncing back is that you know what you're going back to, and you can immediately address the need and reinstate routines previously in place. You can evaluate what worked before and reinforce those things.

As a coping mechanism, bouncing back can be positive. So can bouncing forward. Here we're talking about using the experience of a crisis or challenge to grow stronger, be more capable, build new skills, and implement positive change or growth. Bouncing forward entails transformation, improvement, innovation, and long-term advancement, and it often brings with it a recognition of other risks and issues that might become future crises. It helps you anticipate those crises. It requires you to reflect, learn, and embrace change, to set new goals and recognize and build resilience skills within the group.

What does bouncing forward look like? Someone who is bouncing forward from losing their job will use that experience to further their education, skills, and overall career growth, achieving profound personal fulfillment as a result. They will look forward toward new accomplishments, always keeping one eye on their bigger why and another on greater outcomes. Remarkably, many people use a job transition to realign and produce a more satisfying life for themselves. An organization facing financial crisis, that desires to bounce forward, might need to implement new technologies and business models that improve its efficiency and market position, which in turn can lead to a more competitive organization.

So how can we develop grit?

1. **Set long-term goals that engage your passion.** Your goals must be realistic, and they must emanate from your passion. Break down that passion. Articulate it in a way that provides you with long-term motivation. When you do, you'll realize that even failures will help you succeed. Take a moment and look back at all the things you've gone through in your life, the lessons you've learned, and how your story has shaped your future. Notice when you demonstrated grit in the past. What were the characteristics that enabled your grit? What objectives engendered your passion? What can you do to reclaim that level of grit?

2. **Develop habits that foster perseverance.** Maintaining a positive attitude, staying focused on your goals, embracing challenges rather than running from them, being willing to learn and recognizing how to develop your future, visualizing

success—all constitute smart habits for someone determined to exhibit grit. Flex your self-discipline, which will help you develop and stick with a positive routine. Delay gratification. Be patient and persistent. Seek support and feedback, network and mentorship. Celebrate success. Acknowledge your individual strengths. Engage in regular reflection and adaptive strategies. What goals have you noticed reinforce your willingness to stick to the task and see it through to the end? What do these goals have in common? How can you leverage that again to build grit for current projects and accountabilities?

For some of us, grit takes time to develop. But it's available to anyone willing to work for it. We need only summon the same courage it took us to imagine big dreams and pursue lofty goals. Your grit level as a leader is a predictor of success—for yourself and your team.

Identify your personal mind traps. We all have hot buttons or triggers that can set us off. Some people know what our buttons are and want to push them. Recognize yours so you can consciously manage them. Recognize when you fall into the thinking traps previously explored: jumping to conclusion, tunnel vision, catastrophizing, minimizing, all-or-nothing thinking, personalizing everything, blaming, and so forth. Go back, review the thinking traps we've explored, and determine which ones are your natural hot buttons. You'll be a better leader if you know and can manage yours.

Develop grit. As a leader, you have an accountability to build your grit and help your team build theirs. You can do that by developing the habits that foster perseverance: embracing challenges, learning from failure, and visualizing success. Practice self-discipline and delayed gratification, and celebrate success. Do all of that, and you'll notice grit developing in yourself and your team.

For additional resources to support you on these vital signs, visit
vitalsigns-book/resources.

As a physician leader, I've come to understand that a strong, diverse professional network is essential—not optional—for leading effectively in today's health-care environment. I've intentionally built relationships with key individuals from across the health system and medical school who each enrich my understanding of the overall operation. They are critical stakeholders to my success. Being relatively new to my role, I have assembled a top-notch executive team to help me define clinical, educational, and operational strategies and priorities for the department. I often supplement this team with regional and system clinical and operational leaders. These mentors and advisers understand the daily pressures and aren't afraid to share their candid feedback, especially when I'm facing difficult decisions.

In recent years, I added an executive coach to that circle, and it's been one of the best investments I've made in my leadership development. My coach challenges my thinking, helps me reflect on my blind spots, and keeps me focused on long-term development, not just day-to-day problem-solving.

Leadership can be isolating, but a strong personal and professional network turns that isolation into collaboration—and reminds you that you're part of something larger than yourself.

—Summary of interview with a physician leader: Academic Surgical Chair

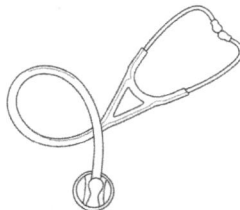

The T-eam-
Supported Leader

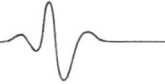

"Leading without a support network is like trying
to dance the cha-cha solo."
—ChatGPT

PRESENTING SYMPTOMS ADDRESSED IN THIS CHAPTER

Resisting advice.   Feeling alone.

Unable/unwilling to adapt.   Trouble listening.

Not seen as a team player.   Out of touch.

Difficulty with boss.   Judgmental.

L eadership is a journey, and it's best traveled with others. It's not a solo task. A leader isn't measured by their capacity to go it alone. A leader is judged by their ability to organize robust networks, which not only ensure that we have guidance and support but also provide strength, insight, directives, and motivation for the group.

The cowboy mentality of leading the charge and taking the hill alone is widely popular in movies. In practice, leadership is lonely, difficult work. Who you select as your support network is a critical decision. Select the right people, and they will provide you both with the updraft and the safety net for your accension into leadership. Select the wrong folks, and you tie a weight around your waist that will hamper your climb.

When I travel in unfamiliar areas, I often hire a guide. On separate trips, I hired a personal guide to take me as a tourist to the Great Wall in China, the Taj Mahal in India, Petra in Jordan, the Christ the Redeemer statue in Brazil, the Coliseum in Rome, and the Holy Lands in Israel. Although each guide required a (surprisingly) small investment, the value of their experience and insights greatly improved my understanding of history, my personal safety, and my enjoyment in witnessing these wonders of the ancient world. Perhaps I could have made my way on my own through the maze of travel arrangements and throngs of people to experience these wonders, but the value of each guide's support and direction vastly improved my experience. The amazing thing about these guides—the really good ones—is that they've built relationships with vendors, security guards, and local citizens that can greatly benefit you as their client. They provide access to those special places and special moments the crowds will never experience.

> A leader is judged by their ability to organize robust networks, which not only ensure that we have guidance and support but also provide strength, insight, directives, and motivation for the group.

On your leadership journey, you have the same decision to make. Will you try to make it on your own, or will you invest in the relationships that can vastly improve your understanding, safety, and enjoyment? Who are the guides that can assist you on that journey? What knowledge and experience do they have to share? How can they provide some protection and comfort in unfamiliar regions? What relationships can they bring to bear to assist you on your journey?

As we think about this final element of the leader's HEART, we must address how we build the support systems (team) needed to help us excel personally and as leaders.

VITAL SIGN NO. 1
NETWORK STRENGTH

What is a network? A collection of resources, individuals, and groups that provide access to knowledge, expertise, and feedback, all of which are critically important to a leader. By engaging a network, a leader can learn best practices, industry standards, and what has worked for other leaders. That's because a network provides opportunities for collaboration, information sharing, synergistic conversations, and partnerships. It provides feedback on a leader's ideas, perspectives, and actions, and that feedback can be constructive while helping to narrow gaps in skills and experience. A network provides support and encouragement, even and especially during challenging times. As I like to say, leadership is lonely, leadership is challenging, and leadership is lonelier during challenging times. It's essential to have someone there to support us, cheer our achievements, celebrate milestones, reinforce our confidence, and motivate us to keep moving, attacking the problem, and leading even during challenges and crises.

> By engaging a network, a leader can learn best practices, industry standards, and what has worked for other leaders.

Networks encourage us to grow personally and professionally. They give us opportunities to support others. And they help us build our reputation, which is built not only on what we say and do but on who we associate with and how we interact with others. Finally, networks provide us with opportunities to influence, learn, share, and challenge ourselves, and those opportunities might lead to new roles or new jobs. Networks often act as referrals for us.

Who should you include in your network? I always suggest starting with your personal support network. Although friends and family might not be directly related to your professional life, they're part of who you are and what you bring to leadership. Sometimes your friends and family will provide support, and sometimes they will offer advice, which might prove useful or misguided. The objective is to find moral and emotional support—a grounding point, if you will—for your leadership. Your personal network should consist of people who support who you are and what you're trying to accomplish as a leader.

Who else can you add to your network? Consider the following:

1. **Industry peers and colleagues.** Your current and/or former colleagues with whom you maintain a relationship know what you're working through or with, understand your industry, and can be supportive of your goals.

2. **Industry competitors.** You need not share industry secrets to gain insights from others in the industry who understand your challenges and objectives. They might attack the job in a different way, and they might offer different products or services from which you can learn and model.

3. **Mentors and advisers.** We'll explore this in more depth below, but these experienced professionals can offer you guidance, advice, and knowledge.

4. **Industry leaders and influencers.** Follow and connect with thought leaders in your network. Consider the recognized "influencers" in your profession. You can learn from their experience and exposures. Your network grows as theirs grows.

5. **Professional associations and groups.** Association members and special interest groups can help you build your knowledge as well as your network.

6. **Clients and partners.** Current and past clients, business partners, suppliers, and other people you've developed relationships with through the organization can also become part of your support network.

7. **Educators and trainers.** Local educational institutions, including those you may not have personally attended, can help you build access to a knowledge base, new research, and the latest technology through education and training delivery. Connect with professors, instructors, and training providers.

8. **Industry service providers.** Recognize what the vendors and suppliers in your industry have to offer. They can provide unique perspectives as part of your network.

9. **Peers in adjacent fields.** Organizations like Vistage and TED bring together CEOs from various industries to participate in discussion groups. Their group objective is to give CEOs the chance to talk to other CEOs outside their industry about their common experience as a chief executive officer. There's something very powerful about the ability to talk confidentially and candidly to others who face the same role challenges but who aren't direct competitors. That's because the CEO of another organization, even in another industry, will face the same challenges that you face. This is not just true for CEOs. For example, although I might be in the health-care market and you might be in manufacturing, we might have several things in common as procurement leaders. If you're a neurosurgeon, you might want to add to your network someone in orthopedics or nursing. Such networks can be useful for understanding situations, gathering feedback based on ideas and challenges, and building influence pools. When you're

trying to execute a new idea, having people that can support you outside of your department but within your organization can prove extremely powerful. Or you can look outside of your organization for those kinds of influence leaders.

As we explore these different kinds of networks, we must understand our objectives for each network and for each potential member of each network. We might not treat everyone in a particular network exactly the same way because of competitive issues, experience differences, or other reasons.

So how do you build a professional network? The first thing you must do is define what your goals are for your network. What are you trying to achieve? Are you trying to gather advisers around you? Are you trying to increase your knowledge? Are you trying to find individuals to collaborate and partner with? What is the purpose of your network? Are you trying to gain more visibility? Are you seeking new career growth? Your objective for a network will influence how you shape that network.

> We must understand our objectives for each network and for each potential member of each network.

Take a moment to look at the individuals who have influenced your perceptions, attitudes, and behaviors. Make them a part of your network. Connect. Reconnect with professors, with former coworkers, with people you respect. Look for people who are open to sharing their expertise and what they've learned, and look for those who've done the work you're attempting to do. If you're a new hospital administrator, look for people who led hospitals in the past. A client of mine, upon taking on a new leadership role, reached out to the previous leaders who had held that role, some of whom had left the company, to learn from their experiences and build a network in the process.

Start local. Look for local resources: local coaches, local educators, local networks that already exist. Build your network around you and then expand from there, moving to regional, national, and even international contacts, if appropriate. And remember that with the internet, everyone's local. Local simply means someone you can gain access to quickly. That someone might live and work outside of your city, region, or country. If they're easy to access, they're local.

And don't forget that *you* can provide opportunity and enrichment to others as well. Who can you help while expanding your network? Who faces similar challenges in their job or organization? Participate in conferences and podcasts. Read books and periodicals. Help connect others in your industry who might be able to help each other. What's good for your network is good for you.

Let's take a closer look at building your network of advisers. Consider these three different types of advisers: bosses, mentors, and what I like to call your personal board of directors.

No one, save perhaps a spouse or close friend, will have more influence on your success and growth as a leader than your boss.

As a formal supervisor within the organizational hierarchy, your boss sets expectations, helps you manage your work, and evaluates your individual performance. No one, save perhaps a spouse or close friend, will have more influence on your success and growth as a leader than your boss. Your relationship with your boss tends to be transactional, performance-oriented, and focused on day-to-day tasks and the achievement of specific goals. When your boss offers feedback or opportunities, there's an expectation that you'll act accordingly. Typically, the boss's feedback is performance-related and is delivered via a performance review, job description, or meeting that is geared toward specific goals and outcomes. A boss's feedback can also take the form of a promotion, salary increase, or increase in job variety.

Ultimately, your boss has direct responsibility for your outcomes and is thus a crucial member of your network.

So how do you go about building a good relationship with your boss? Start by defining your goals. Clarify what you hope to achieve from the relationship. Are you seeking clarity regarding your account-abilities? Do you want to have input into the development of your position?

Next, aim for a win-win relationship. So many of my clients expect their boss to enable them to win but forget that part of their responsibility is to work directly to enable wins for their boss. As you think about the win-win, think about what you can gain from the relationship *and* what you can give. What can you share with your boss? How can you make their job easier? You can also help them take responsibility for your performance and development. Many leaders don't understand how to enable growth in others, but if you're taking accountability for your personal leadership, you can help your boss enable your growth. You can help define SMART (Specific, Measurable, Achievable, Relevant, and Time-Bound) goals for per-formance, ask the difficult questions about the role you're to play (questions your boss might not think to ask), and help them clarify success. Consider your goals for the contribution of learning together and include them in your definitions of this win-win relationship.

You can enhance your development, not just your performance, by asking your boss to clarify the goals, metrics, and outcomes you're moving toward. Ask them to help shape the boundaries of your job. If your boss doesn't have the skills or experience to do so, remember that as a leader, you ultimately have the accountability to make sure those things are clear. Your boss should know not only your aspirations and career goals but also the opportunities and challenges you face on a day-to-day basis. Seek regular feedback, act on it, and tell them you acted on it. These are the behaviors of a leader who is leveraging their boss as an adviser. You can even arrange developmental meetings with your boss to discuss your goals and your outcomes. Just remember that in most situations we're hired to help the boss accomplish their defined responsibilities—just like the people who work for us are hired to help us execute *our* responsibilities—so be careful not to make this a one-way conversation.

What else can you do to strengthen your relationship with your boss?

1. **Ask your boss for stretch assignments.** Encourage them to give you new responsibilities and accountabilities, and tell them what you need to handle them.

2. **Learn from their leadership style.** You can observe and analyze their leadership, which means learning good things to emulate and bad things to avoid. Both are educational.

3. **Demonstrate accountability and growth.** Clarify together your scope of accountability today and those areas of accountability you hope to grow into over time. Help your boss lead you by being clear on your aspirations and expectations while being open to adjustment based on their feedback and advice.

4. **Ask for what you need from them if you're not getting it.** Your boss might not know how to lead you. You might need to lead them toward leading you better. Be patient, and be responsible for your own development. Take personal accountability, and let them know how they can help you produce more.

5. **Actively engage in and be prepared for meetings and discussions.** Consider ideas ahead of time. Back in the day, leaders often said, "Don't bring me problems without a solution." There's some validity to that. My job as a leader isn't just to highlight the problems; it's to help solve them.

6. **Be receptive to your boss's feedback.** Be open to criticism. Doing so takes courage and self-awareness.

Some bosses want to be more than your boss. They want to be your *mentor*. My advice? Know the difference between the two. A mentor is typically an experienced individual who offers expert guidance and support. Unlike your boss, they don't have a formal, *hierarchical* relationship with you. Instead, they're a trusted adviser who acts as a sounding board and offers advice without expectations. A mentor gives you feedback and the accountability to decide what to do with it. The relationship is different because a mentor is typically focused more on your personal growth and learning than immediate performance. They're interested in your long-term development.

Some organizations provide formal mentoring, with mixed results. Some are quite successful, particularly when the mentee has the opportunity to interview and select their mentor. Along with having a say over who mentors them, the mentee can gauge the level of chemistry they have with their prospective mentor. But formal programs often struggle assigning mentors to groups or individuals. All they can do is look at characteristics and estimate who might work well together. Sometimes that approach works, but most of the time, it's less effective than something more organic and informal.

Again, a mentor offers feedback from a developmental perspective. The goal is guidance and improvement, not specific outcomes. Although personally involved, a mentor typically doesn't take responsibility for the relationship. As you would with a boss, aim for a win-win relationship with your mentor, and clarify what you want out of that relationship. Are you seeking career advice? Skill development? Look for someone with the experience base you're hoping to grow.

When assessing a potential mentor relationship, don't forget to assess your compatibility. You might work well with one person but not someone else. Look for someone with a complementary style and similar expectations. Before you approach them, do some research and prepare for the conversation. Tell them what you're trying to achieve and why you'd like for them to be your mentor, and make that contact as personal as you can, whether face-to-face or via email or LinkedIn. Perhaps a mutual connection can introduce you. You might say something like, "Hi. I've been following your work, and I'm impressed by your accomplishments. I'm hoping to improve my abilities in this area and would greatly appreciate the opportunity to learn from your experience."

Check to see if a formal mentoring program is already in place. A program at the local university hospital, for example, might link you with a prospective physician mentor. If there's no formal program in place, define your expectations and the structure you seek, meet with your prospective mentor to discuss your goals, and get their input on their goals for the mentorship. Perhaps you'll agree to meet once a month over lunch, and ahead of each meeting, you'll provide in advance a couple of topics that you wish to discuss. Set those goals, and establish a plan and definitive schedule. Be careful not to expect too much from a mentor. Most won't be available to you 24/7, although they'll probably be amenable to an impromptu phone call now and then. Be sure to actively engage and prepare. You're asking somebody to give you their greatest gift: their time and experience. So make sure you treat it as a gift and reciprocate accordingly.

After you've met with them, reflect on what they said and adapt your approach as needed. In some cases, you might choose not to heed their advice; that's your decision. This isn't a teacher-student relationship. This is a mentor-mentee relationship, a colleague-to-colleague relationship. In such a relationship, you decide how you will use the information you glean.

The idea behind a mentorship is to build a long-lasting relationship. It will evolve over time, and the topic of conversation will change as the relationship grows. Look for ways you can offer support and engage your mentor. It might be something completely different, like teaching them to play guitar or helping them with something of interest to them. Regardless, find ways to give back to the relationship.

Although a mentor is different from a boss, the two roles share several things in common:

- Both provide varied insights.
- Both will challenge you to think differently.
- Both boast a different experience base and thus can make a unique contribution to your development. Be open to their insights and specialized knowledge.
- Both can help you make better decisions.
- Both can hold you accountable, with mentors acting as accountability partners.
- Both can provide access to their networks, which in turn will bring new opportunities, more visibility, and perhaps even new resources.
- Both can support your personal and professional growth.
- Both can help you develop your strategic plan, offering actionable advice along the way and helping with problem-solving because they bring a range of problem-solving approaches and creative solutions. Working collaboratively with them leverages your collective experience to produce something new and unique.
- Both can offer reassurance as you grapple with tough challenges, and both can validate and confirm your decisions afterward.
- Both can provide you and your team with continuous feedback and recommendations for improvement.

Once you've solidified your relationships with your boss and your mentor, I recommend establishing a personal board of directors. It's become popular, particularly for someone managing their own business, to maintain a board of directors. But you don't need to own a business or run an organization to benefit from the knowledge of those around you. Think about those people in your life that you can assemble periodically for a short, focused conversation. As you would at a board meeting, you can use the conversation to gather their advice, ideas, reactions, and support. Keep the number between three and six people, and meet quarterly to discuss a specific topic that you've prepared ahead of time.

The quality of your network is a predictor of your personal and leadership success.

Start by clarifying your goals. What are you trying to achieve? Career growth? Personal development? Do you need help with building new skills? Strategic decision-making? Then select your personal board members, identifying them based on their ability to help you meet your goal or goals. Seek diversity in background, skills, and viewpoints. If everyone looks and thinks like you, then you really haven't added value with the board. Consider looking at leaders in similar roles in different industries. They can offer different approaches to challenges. After contacting them, tell them what you're trying to do, and make it compelling. A two-hour dinner at a nice restaurant—on you, of course—often makes for a fair trade. Schedule a regular meeting, discussing and creating the agenda ahead of time so they know how to prepare and contribute as best they can. Use each meeting to engage them and learn from them.

Your job here is to ask questions, not to justify or defend your approach. Ideally, you've come prepared with three questions on the agenda. After asking each question, sit back and listen attentively to the discussion that follows. This is your chance to integrate new ideas and important feedback. Even if you don't agree with everything you're hearing, don't waste anyone's time by arguing or trying to defend your position. You're there to learn.

As is the case with your relationships with your mentor and boss, the relationships you form with your personal board of directors will change over time. Some members might come and go based on their needs and yours. You can review and adjust as you go. Be sure to express gratitude to each board member and give them recognition for their help.

The quality of your network is a predictor of your personal and leadership success. As the knight at the end of the movie *Indiana Jones and the Last Crusade* advised, "Choose wisely."

VITAL SIGN NO. 2
STAKEHOLDER AWARENESS

When I talk about stakeholders, I'm talking about the other people in your sphere of influence with whom you can build a teaming relationship. Team members, senior leaders within your organization, customers and clients, peers, colleagues, shareholders and investors, regulatory bodies, community, external partners—the list goes on. If you work at a hospital, for example, you're most likely attuned to the communities you serve and endeavor to understand their unique needs. Regardless of where you work or what work you do, you can ponder the same questions. Who will influence the outcomes of yourself and your team? Who will *be influenced by* the outcomes you produce? Those are your stakeholders. Create your list, understand your list, and invest in building relationships with your identified stakeholders.

A stakeholder analysis, a useful tool for many leaders, asks you to ponder which stakeholders can help you succeed as a leader.[31] You can group them by name, by the role they play in the organization, or by a particular category. Next, think about what those stakeholders value. Some stakeholders might be financially oriented. Others might be patient- or client-centric. Some might be revenue- or results-oriented. Others might be reputation-oriented. Thinking about your stakeholders' values does two things: First, it helps you better understand them and their perspective and therefore their feedback; second, it teaches you how to work with them, because now you understand their priorities and can emphasize their priorities as you're talking about and working through different leadership challenges.

For the last part of a stakeholder analysis, ask yourself, "How will they impact my leadership?" Some will have little impact. Others will have a monumental impact in certain situations but not in others.

Consider the question carefully. Answering it will help you recognize that, again, leaders don't lead by themselves. They invest in a network of people around them, and stakeholders are part of that investment. You must understand what the stakeholders need, what they consider important, and how they're going to influence your leadership responsibilities and outcomes.

The stakeholders which contribute to the success of your team, and you as its leader, will be unique to your team, its outcomes, and its mission. Stakeholders vary based on each individual project. If your team is accountable for implementing a new accounting software across a multilocation organization, the stakeholders for that project might include senior location leadership, central IT, local IT, central accounting, local accounting resources that will enter data, those that prepare financial reports, those that receive reports, and so on. If you're in a client-facing organization, a stakeholder analysis will help you identify not only the customers but the characteristics of those customers that influence their buying decision. Marketing groups go as far as to create stakeholder personas that summarize the unique priorities, preferences, and objectives for product use or service selection for different market segments to help bring to life the diversity and needs of customers for the product design and sales teams. The same analysis is a powerful tool to help leaders and their teams understand who influences their success. Once a stakeholder analysis is defined and analyzed, the team better understands their customers, their suppliers, the decision-makers, and the organizational leadership influencing project objectives and daily decisions.

> You must understand what the stakeholders need, what they consider important, and how they're going to influence your leadership responsibilities and outcomes.

I'm surprised when a leader hesitates in their response to the core question, "Who are the stakeholders of your team's success?" An effective leader will know who those individuals and groups (both internal and external) are that directly impact success in their organization, their department, their specific products and services, and their priority projects. That knowledge is critical to obtaining those success-related goals.

Let's consider carefully how you'll communicate with your stakeholders. Too often leaders assume that a single message will connect with all stakeholders. Rarely is that true. A single message might be too detailed for some and too basic for others. Go back to your stakeholder analysis: the list of individuals, their goals and priorities, and how they might influence your project. Now consider adding a fourth item: the best way to communicate with them. Some groups might prefer that you talk with them face-to-face. Others will be fine with an email. Some might expect an organized PowerPoint. Others might prefer a small discussion group. You can select the ideal form of communication based on the work you've already done on your stakeholder analysis. Recognize that, as is the case with their unique preferences and priorities, a stakeholder group has a best way (or ways) to communicate effectively with them. And recognize that the focus on stakeholders shifts the focus from us to them. It changes our priorities to what might be most efficient for us to what is most effective for them.

> Too often leaders assume that a single message will connect with all stakeholders. Rarely is that true.

Let's take a moment to discuss one of the most critical stakeholder groups in a leader's success, the leadership support team. With whom do you share a leadership responsibility for your team? Typically, these are your direct reports who also have leadership accountabilities for other groups of individual contributors (e.g., chiefs of different functions within the department). In a matrixed organization, this team might also include members or representatives from other groups: central administration, HR, finance, etc. Together, this group represents your leadership team and is responsible for shaping policy and process and ensuring execution of the larger entity or organization.

Sometimes we inherit such groups, particularly if we're new to the leadership role, but over time, we have the opportunity to reshape them. I encourage you to think carefully about the makeup of this group and about ensuring everyone shares a mutual purpose. Each member should contribute experience, knowledge, and strengths to the overall team accountability. Recognize the groups/functions they represent, and help everyone understand your expectations for membership in the group. Ideally, group members will be empowered to challenge each other and will be expected to support each other, even in difficult decisions, to build unity in support of your common mission. Invest in shaping and developing this team, because it will play a critical role in its success—and yours. Your team is the link between strategy and execution, and ultimately it has the accountability for executing the decisions and strategies of the leadership team. Make sure this is the right group. A team that boasts a diversity of experience and thought can help you make the best possible decisions. Sometimes, a smaller leader's council (a subset of the larger leadership team) is appropriate to provide you direct council and support, even before issues are addressed in the larger leadership team setting. Again, choose wisely.

Invest in your leadership team's stakeholders so that they understand the boundaries of their individual roles. Job clarity is critical here. Let them know how they can collaborate and where they can provide entrepreneurial ideas and perspectives. Where do you want them to push the envelope, and where should they show restraint? Clarifying such things helps them contribute, and doing so will not only help you as you select individuals but also as you encourage them to collaborate and work with each other.

Your leadership team must be aligned with the organization's vision, values, and mission, all of which they should embrace as part of the team leadership. You can also help explain what those values mean in practice to you as the leader and how they can support and contribute to them.

> A team—and a leader, for that matter—is only successful to the extent the service it delivers contributes to meeting the desires and expectations of its stakeholders.

Take some time to get to know the leaderships styles of your leadership team stakeholders. If you need to rethink foundational issues, revisit the topics we've discussed in previous chapters. Understanding the organization's culture and strategy (H), the level of engagement (E), the degree of accountability (A), and the amount of resilience (R) will help you in your evaluation as you ponder not only selection but also the operation itself. When you evaluate teamwork (T), you'll want to take a closer look at team dynamics, which we'll discuss in more depth later in this book. A team—and a leader, for that matter—is only successful to the extent the service it delivers contributes to meeting the desires and expectations of its stakeholders. It pays to understand your stakeholders.

VITAL SIGN NO. 3
FEEDBACK SYSTEMS

The next vital sign of leadership HEART health assesses the feedback systems and your ability as a communicator. Whether you're interacting with your network, advisers, or stakeholders, strive to be a good communicator. We begin communicating the moment we're born, but that doesn't make communication easy or simple. Every communication includes a sender and a receiver of a message, and everyone who sends a message faces the same challenge: making sure the receiver understands it in the way it was intended to be understood.

Countless things can get in the way of effective communication. These interferences to good communication can emanate from the sender, the receiver, the context, and even the physical environment. Psychologist and UCLA professor Albert Mehrabian illustrated in his research that a tiny fraction of our communication actually comes from words themselves.[32] The rest is delivered via tone, body language, facial expressions, and so forth. Our reception of a message, meanwhile, also affects how we interpret it. If we're distracted, we can miss the meaning of what was intended to be shared. And if we've already made up our mind, a message might fall on deaf ears. We can have two people—a boss and an employee, for example—describing a disciplinary discussion in wildly disparate terms. The boss insists that they made the need for connection and potential disciplinary action clear and that the employee clearly understood it, yet the employee counters that the message was unclear and that they didn't understand it.

Although we would love to believe it and often insist to our significant others that we are good listeners, few of us really are. While we might physically hear something, we often allow our own judgment and selective filters to impact interpretations without checking to ensure that our interpretation aligns with the intended message. It's amazing how often what we receive doesn't match the intent of what was sent. Prejudging and filtering, rather than simply listening to understand intent, takes place in the workplace too. Most managers find it challenging to withhold judgment while listening. That's because, like the rest of us, they often start thinking about their response before the other person has finished making their point. Or they make a judgment about the value and content of the communication before the speaker has finished. Add distractions like environmental, physical, emotional, or societal noise, and it's a wonder anything is communicated at all.

> Communication is perhaps the most central element of personal development and team building. An investment in building our communication abilities always pays dividends.

The goal of effective communication is shared meaning. When I communicate something to you, I want to know if you actually heard it the way I intended it. We've all been in a situation where someone takes offense at something we said because they heard it differently than we meant it. The magic of feedback is that it's one of the few ways we can actually ensure shared meaning between the sender and the receiver. If you send me a message, I can offer feedback to ensure that I understand what it is you're trying to say. This gives you an opportunity to clarify exactly what you mean. Such a back-and-forth, give-and-take process allows us to refine communication until we've arrived at a shared meaning.

A sender can improve communication by asking the recipient to parrot their communication. "What did you hear me say?" Or the recipient can do so unprompted. "This is what I hear you saying." If we're misaligned, we'll discover it as we narrow the gap between how the message was intended and how it was received. Taking this extra step to ensure that we're on the same page has the potential to all but eliminate misunderstandings and confusion. No one will need to fall back on, "But you never told me that," if we insist on clear communication up front.

I can identify and assemble an extraordinary network of advisers and stakeholders, but if I fail to communicate effectively, no one will be able to help me become a better leader or move toward better outcomes. Communication is perhaps the most central element of personal development and team building. An investment in building our communication abilities always pays dividends.

When it comes to receiving feedback, we can be proactive in the following ways:

1. **Ask for it.** A manager at a respiratory ventilator company developed the habit of carrying three-by-five cards in his pocket to remind him to ask for feedback from his employees. At the beginning of each week, he picked five individuals to query and wrote their names on the cards. In the event that he forgot to carry the cards with him, he invited his employees to remind him, offering a dollar to anyone who did so. This turned the exercise into a game—and ensured that he collected a steady stream of feedback from everyone in the organization.

2. **Practice active listening.** Most of us find this challenging, because our first impulse is always to respond before we understand. Override that and take the time to comprehend what someone is expressing. Stephen Covey implores us to, "Seek first to understand, then to be understood."[33] Ask for clarification if you don't understand something. Never assume you know what someone intends to say before they finish saying it. Ask for examples, details, and so forth when someone offers you feedback, thus providing you with additional data

from which to seek shared meaning. And take a moment to reflect back to the sender what you believe you heard. Doing so confirms your understanding and offers them the opportunity to correct or clarify if your reflection is inaccurate.

3. **Explore how someone's feedback makes you feel.** This requires courage, because often someone's feedback generates powerful emotions in us, including anger, frustration, and joy. Take a moment to study your feelings. Doing so will help you understand what you can do with that feedback. Usually when I find myself frustrated by feedback, it's because the feedback is true, I know it's true, and I should have already fixed it.

4. **Gather multiple perspectives.** What you'll find is that one person might be unhappy about an initiative or project while others are happy about it. When we hear from multiple people, we can look for trends and for things that are consistently mentioned. We can then act to address those trends and shared concerns.

And here are a few things we *shouldn't* do when receiving feedback:

1. **Don't attempt to justify your actions.** When someone gives us feedback, it's easy to say, "Well, I did that because of this or that." While that might be true, it doesn't add value to the conversation. In fact, it tends to shut down the conversation. If you make excuses every time you receive feedback, people will stop offering it.

2. **Don't apologize or promise you'll never do it again.** This happens a lot during performance reviews. A leader gives someone feedback about something they need to improve,

and the employee responds by saying, "That'll never happen again." That's a dangerous thing to say, because we can't always meet such expectations. Just listen.

3. **Don't shoot the messenger.** Are you tempted to punish someone when they give you bad feedback? Resist that temptation. Instead, listen and absorb what they have to say. It might hurt to hear it, especially if it's untrue or unjustified, but your goal is to keep open the lines of communication, not close them.

4. **Don't discount feedback because of the source.** Some of the best feedback you'll ever receive might come from an easily dismissed source. If you're a physician, you can still learn from a nurse, anesthesiologist, or patient. When we discount feedback based on who offered it, we need to explore our prejudices. Ultimately, we might choose not to act on someone's feedback, but we owe it to ourselves and our team to at least explore it. If we react in kneejerk fashion, we might regret it later as we ponder the feedback in more depth. It's best to hear something, consider it, and then decide. The alternative is akin to "Ready, fire, aim!"

Giving feedback, meanwhile, affords us the chance to establish and review expectations. It can also help us motivate people and build energy. You can be proactive in how you give feedback in several ways:

1. **Intend to be helpful.** Have you ever been tempted to give someone feedback to prove a point, demonstrate you were right, or knock someone down a peg or two? To give someone feedback just to make yourself look or feel better is selfish—and not something an effective leader does.

2. **Ignore distractions.** You're sitting in your office, about to give someone feedback, and the phone rings. What do you do? Unless it's a high-priority phone call, let it go through to voice mail. If you pick up, you've communicated that the phone is more important than the person sitting across from you.

3. **Be specific.** Provide details and recent examples. Nothing is more frustrating than receiving feedback that is too vague or that repeats old tapes. Help someone learn from and apply your feedback by using specific recent examples.

4. **Focus on what you can observe when providing feedback.** Judging motives implies you know how someone thinks and understand their intentions. This is a dangerous game, because it quickly can become a debate about intentions—an argument you can't win. Judging another's motives often blocks their ability to hear your feedback. Rather than implying motives, stick to the actions you observed and the impact of those actions. Shape solutions through actions as well. This way you can both witness the improvement (or lack thereof).

5. **Use "I" statements.** When discussing someone's behavior or action, you can share how it impacted you. Saying, "I felt disrespected when you came to the meeting late," is very different than saying, "You intended to disrespect me by coming to the meeting late." Using "I" statements allows you to own your own feedback and focuses the discussion. It also helps you avoid assigning the source of the feedback to some nebulous group (i.e., "We all feel"), for which you most likely don't have authority to speak.

6. **Clarify all of your expectations.** Ask for acknowledgment of the content and implications of what you shared. Remember that the goal of communication is shared meaning, so make sure they understood your intent.

Consider the leader who is concerned that a powerful colleague is attempting to sabotage her and undermine her leadership. During a recent exchange with the aforementioned colleague, she said, "You're always doing things to cause me pain and make my job difficult." Can you see how this reaction violates several of the principles outlined above? Even if her accusations are true, such statements rarely lead to a fruitful discussion or outcome. In fact, there's no information in her accusation about how to move forward. A better option would be for her to say something like this: "You went around me and spoke directly to the executive director about a previously unexpressed concern. This made me feel like I was being painted in a bad light. I also didn't feel like my ability to address the issue directly was respected." She addresses the issue, tying it to a specific behavior and her specific concerns. Now they both have something specific to exchange.

VITAL SIGN NO. 4
DERAILER RISKS

The Center for Creative Leadership (CCL) has identified what they call "career derailers."[34] Let's look at what their research of reviewing the behaviors of tens of thousands of leaders uncovered. The first career derailer is failing to meet business objectives. It is not surprising that if I consistently miss business objectives, I'll likely derail my career. The second career derailer is when I focus too narrowly on the functional/technical area of my daily work without recognizing how that work fits into the larger operational systems of the organization. If I'm so focused on the specifics of what I do that I don't recognize the required coordination and resulting impacts of my work upstream and downstream in the process, I can derail my career. For example, If I'm a cancer researcher so focused on "the science" that I don't invest time in building relationships and understanding the unique needs of my clinician partners and their patients, I'll likely struggle to build support for my required clinical trials.

The other three career derailers all relate to leading teams:

- **Difficulty in building and leading a team.** Someone who struggles to build or lead a team won't understand the social and performance dynamics of their team, and/or how to motivate their team.
- **Difficulty with interpersonal relationships.** An effective leader is adaptive to the interpersonal dynamics within the team. An ineffective leader, in contrast, tends to blame problems on personality conflicts. They often lack emotional intelligence, not recognizing the impact their behaviors have on those around them. Such a leader doesn't understand how to build an environment where relationships flourish.

- **Difficulty changing and adapting.** Changes and adaptations almost always unfold in the context of a team. Leaders who are unable to work with their team to adapt and change tend to derail their own careers.

In his book *What Got You Here Won't Get You There*, Marshall Goldsmith identifies twenty ineffective habits that prevent leaders from growing, especially early in their career.[35] As you climb the corporate ladder and/or assume bigger responsibilities in your organization, it's tempting to rely on the habits that helped you succeed as an inexperienced employee or first-line leader. But doing so, Goldsmith illustrates, isn't always effective. Attention to detail might serve you well as an individual contributor or first-line supervisor, for example, but the same habit can work against you now that you're a CEO. Your new leadership position requires you to move swiftly through large quantities of data, and you're going to have to make corporate-wide decisions while operating in ambiguity. Can you do either if you're focused on small-bore issues?

> There are times in your leadership journey when you need to not only develop new skills but leave some behaviors behind.

Listed below are several—but not all—of the ineffectual habits Goldsmith explores. There are times in your leadership journey when you need to not only develop new skills but leave some behaviors behind. As you think about working with your team and serving as its leader, recognize that the following behaviors have the potential to slow or even prevent your growth:

1. **Winning too much.** Do you need to win at all costs, even when it doesn't matter? A leader that argues trivial points is attempting to demonstrate to their team that they understand

the situation and are in charge. But what that leader really conveys is a petty, small-minded nature.

2. **Adding too much value.** Some leaders get in their own way because they have to be the one who answers every question and solves every problem. This is a challenge for smart people, in particular. Engineers, scientists, physicians, and surgeons are trained to solve problems, which can prevent them from allowing other people to find the solution. An effective leader, remember, encourages everyone on the team to contribute and grow.

3. **Passing judgment.** Judging others usually means imposing standards on them. Every leader must make judgment calls when the moment demands it. But if you make those judgments too quickly or without the appropriate information, you risk thwarting or misdirecting your team.

4. **Making destructive comments.** Sarcasm and cutting remarks never contribute positively to the situation. Some of us take great pride in our ability to have the quick sarcastic quip. Too often those comments, although perhaps intended to introduce humor, cut others down, particularly the boss or the company/organization. As you grow in responsibility, making destructive comments becomes a limiting factor, because your influence is damaged every time you deliver such remarks, even at the water cooler, company picnic, or a social event outside of company activities.

5. **Starting with "no," "but," or "however."** Doing so implies your team member is wrong and risks shutting down dialogue and a potential exchange of ideas. We need to be aware of how we interact with our team and how we encourage each

member. If you immediately reply to someone's feedback with "no," "but," or "however," you diminish their desire to give you important feedback. We don't always agree with another's perspective or recommendations, but we can demonstrate that we value their contribution, perspective, or courage to share. Look for the 10 percent of their idea that you find valuable and start there to acknowledge that they are adding value to the conversation. Some leaders prefer the "Yes, and . . ." approach, which acknowledges the value of another's ideas while redirecting the conversation. A simple "Thank you for sharing your perspective" before we react to their expressed comments also works to reinforce someone's contribution without accepting their plan.

6. **Telling the world how smart we are.** In some organizations, groups, or teams, everyone thinks they're smarter than everyone else in the room. In order to prove it, such individuals engage in odd behaviors, level accusations at their colleagues, and participate in counterproductive, counter-collaborative conduct. This is particularly difficult in a room full of extremely smart people vying for reputation and respect from each other. Imagine the potential interaction when a group of world-class physician researchers inhabit the same room. In such cases, an effective leader acknowledges the brain power assembled but focuses on the mission and works to engage each mind while limiting grandstanding and war stories.

7. **Speaking when angry.** Recognize that some of us are more emotionally volatile than others. We can use that volatility as a tool but not as a reaction. A football coach who is always screaming at his players will struggle to get their attention when it really matters.

8. **Being negative.** If you share negative thoughts even when not asked for them, if you're a "negative Nelly," if you view the cup as half empty, your team will struggle. The answer isn't to become artificially optimistic or embrace Pollyannish thinking. Instead, simply train yourself to look for the positive and to share that positivity with and model it for your team.

Three other habits on Goldman's list are withholding information, claiming credit for something someone else did, and overestimating our own contributions. We often engage in such behavior because we think it will help us gain some kind of advantage, but all it does is shrink us in the eyes of our team members. We can overcome such behaviors by aiming for transparency instead.

One of the most guarded secrets of successful leadership is vulnerability. As Brené Brown argues, vulnerability attracts rather than repels people.[36] Why? Because we're all vulnerable, and demonstrating that truth to our network, advisers, and stakeholders, especially while giving and receiving feedback, strengthens our team and our connection to team members. The chief role of a leader is to help their team be accountable, and a leader does that by focusing on the what, not the how. Many of the behaviors that can derail our career are closely related to how we interact and communicate with our team, whether our network, advisers, or stakeholders. If we focus on growth and positive outcomes, we can help everyone around us grow.

PREVENTIVE HEALTH ACTIONS (2-DO'S)
ACTIONS TO TAKE TO ENSURE HEART HEALTH

Conduct a stakeholder analysis. Who are your major stakeholders? You can name them individually or by category. What are they interested in? How do they influence you as a leader? How do they influence your team? Execute and update your stakeholder analysis. It will help you make better decisions as you interact with each stakeholder.

Invest in connections. Think carefully about your support network and invest in it as a leader. Who should you cultivate a connection with? Which advisers should you build your connection with? Who are the stakeholders that you need to build a stronger relationship with? Knowing who the stakeholders are is important. Knowing what their perspectives are is also important. But building in and investing in a relationship is even more important.

For additional resources to support you on these vital signs, visit vitalsigns-book/resources.

Conclusion:

Take Your Pulse

Monitor your HEART health as a leader. Be aware of your engagement, your accountability, your levels of resilience, and the health of your support. Monitor those things not once but often—just as you would your personal health with an Apple watch. Perhaps this book has inspired you to do a deep dive into your HEART health as a leader. I would suggest periodically thinking anew about each component to make sure you're in tune with your HEART health.

Where it exists, address HEART disease. Do so quickly and in a focused way, and look for others who can help you with the process. Go back to your team or network that you've identified. Maybe a coach can help you with a particularly difficult HEART disease. If you diagnose a HEART disease, take the steps necessary to enable your HEART to return to its healthy state. If you're unclear on your values, invest in understanding them. If you don't feel engaged in your current work, explore why that is. If you find yourself avoiding personal accountability for the things that you're called to be accountable for or the responsibility for others' accountability, explore, understand, and diagnose that. Let's get rid of that disease.

Finally, strengthen and protect your HEART from disease that might invade over time. It's not enough to understand the vital signs that measure the health of your HEART. As a leader, you must engage in the exercises and preventive measures that strengthen your HEART, just as you would eat healthy foods, exercise regularly, and get proper rest to care for your physical heart. This book has been designed to not only help you diagnose potential problems within the leader's HEART but to invest in HEART health and provide tips for preventing HEART disease.

As a leader, you must remember that your HEART health matters. Not only to you and your career success but also to your team, your organization, your patients. They want you to have a healthy HEART both for your sake and theirs. You play an important role in the success of your team and your organization. Although it might seem noble to attend first to the HEART health of your team before you address your own, I suggest that when the leader's HEART is diseased, the team's HEART will be ailing as well.

Return to the HEART protocol described in this book often to monitor and maintain HEART health. Visit *Vitalsigns-book.com* for updated treatment options and tools for ensuring a healthy HEART.

I love coaching physician leaders. They understand the importance and priority of healthy behaviors to optimal performance. They are smart, dedicated people doing difficult work and trying their best to positively impact the lives of others. That's exactly how I describe an effective leader: a smart, dedicated person doing difficult work and trying their best to positively impact the lives of others! I hope this resource and the ones on my website, *vitalsigns-book.com*, provide you with the tools necessary to help you make the leadership impact you desire.

The second book of this *Vital Signs* series addresses how to diagnose and treat the HEART of the organization. Together, we'll apply the HEART Protocol to the leadership of organizations. Specifically, we'll discuss the vital signs of health within your organization as we explore how to build:

H-ealthy strategy and supporting culture.
E-ngaged workforce.
A-ccountable team members.
R-esilient systems and staff.
T-eaming behaviors of collaboration.

Join me there.

PRESENTING SYMPTOM CROSS-REFERENCE

This index will help you locate treatment recommendations based on presenting symptom observed.

—⌁—

GUIDE TO HEALTHY LEADERSHIP
Symptoms Cross Reference

PRESENTING SYMPTOM	SEE **HEART** COMPONENT
1. Bored.	E-ngaged
2. Burning out others.	H-ealthy
3. Burnout.	R-esilient
4. Career stagnation.	E-ngaged
5. Decreased job satisfaction.	E-ngaged
6. Difficulty with boss.	T-eam Supported
7. Exaggeration of consequences.	R-esilient
8. Fear of failure.	R-esilient
9. Feeling alone.	T-eam Supported
10. Feeling like a victim.	A-ccountable
11. Feeling out of control.	A-ccountable
12. Feelings of disengagement.	E-ngaged
13. Feelings of frustration.	E-ngaged
14. Heightened tenson.	R-esilient
15. Hiding mistakes.	R-esilient
16. Increased stress.	E-ngaged
17. Judgmental.	T-eam Supported
18. Lack of time for self.	H-ealthy
19. Lack of trust from your staff.	H-ealthy
20. Lack of work-life balance.	H-ealthy

21. Lacking motivation for work.	H-ealthy
22. Looking to pass the buck.	A-ccountable
23. Loss of influence.	E-ngaged
24. Making excuses.	R-esilient
25. Missing personal goals.	A-ccountable
26. Negative thinking.	H-ealthy
27. Not seen as a team player.	T-eam Supported
28. Others complain to you.	A-ccountable
29. Others do not rely on you.	A-ccountable
30. Out of touch.	T-eam Supported
31. Overconfidence.	A-ccountable
32. Overwhelmed.	R-esilient
33. Procrastination.	A-ccountable
34. Pulled in too many directions.	H-ealthy
35. Resisting advice.	T-eam Supported
36. Signs of addiction potential.	H-ealthy
37. Strained relationships.	E-ngaged
38. Too critical of self.	R-esilient
39. Trouble listening.	T-eam Supported
40. Unable/unwilling to adapt.	T-eam Supported

ENDNOTES

1   John C. Maxwell, *The Self-Aware Leader: Play to Your Strengths, Unleash Your Team* (Nashville: HarperCollins Leadership, 2021).

2   Brené Brown, *Dare to Lead: Brave Work. Tough Conversations. Whole Hearts* (Random House, 2018).

3   Peter G. Northouse, *Leadership: Theory and Practice* (SAGE Publications, Inc., 2015).

4   Bill George, *Discover Your True North* (Jossey-Bass, 2015).

5   Stephen Covey, *The 7 Habits of Highly Effective People* (Simon & Schuster, reissue edition, 2020).

6   A. C. Brooks, *From Strength to Strength: Finding Success, Happiness, and Deep Purpose in the Second Half of Life* (Portfolio, 2022).

7   Marshall Goldsmith, *What Got You Here Won't Get You There: How Successful People Become Even More Successful* (Profile Books, 2013).

8   Tara Mohr, *Playing Big: Practical Wisdom for Women Who Want to Speak Up, Create, and Lead* (Avery Publishing Group, 2015).

9   *The Georgia Tech Whistle*, Volume 17, Number 27, September 30, 1991.

10   Peter Salovey and John Mayer coined the term *emotional intelligence* while developing the concepts behind it. Daniel Goleman popularized the idea in his book *Emotional Intelligence: Why It Can Matter More Than IQ* (Bantam, 2005).

11   Shirzad Chamine, *Positive Intelligence: Why Only 20% of Teams and Individuals Achieve Their True Potential and How You Can Achieve Yours* (Greenleaf Book Group Press, 2012).

12   Covey, *The 7 Habits of Highly Effective People.*

13   See https://research.com/education/scientific-benefits-of-gratitude. Also see: Janice Kaplin, *The Gratitude Diaries* (Dutton, 2016).

14   https://www.youtube.com/watch?v=KVjfFN89qvQ

15   Daniel J. Levitin, *I Heard There Was a Secret Chord: Music as Medicine* (New York: W. W. Norton & Company, 2024).

16   Goldsmith, *What Got You Here Won't Get You There: How Successful People Become Even More Successful.*

17 Simon Sinek, *Start with Why: How Great Leaders Inspire Everyone to Take Action* (Portfolio, 2009).

18 Carol S. Dweck, PhD, *Mindset: The New Psychology of Success* (Ballantine Books, 2007).

19 Albert Bandura, *Self-Efficacy: The Exercise of Control* (Worth Publishers, 1997).

20 Covey, *The 7 Habits of Highly Effective People.*

21 See Donald Clifton, *Now, Discover Your Strengths* (Gallup Press, 2020) and *StrengthsFinder 2.0* (Gallup Press, 2007).

22 Gallup, "How Employees' Strengths Make Your Company Stronger" (Gallup.com, 2025). This statistic has been consistently reported across multiple Gallup studies and publications over the years.

23 Roger Connors, Tom Smith, and Craig Hickman, *The Oz Principle: Getting Results Through Individual and Organizational Accountability* (Portfolio, 2010).

24 Angela Duckworth, *Grit: The Power of Passion and Perseverance* (Scribner, 2016).

25 https://www.apa.org/topics/resilience

26 Karen Reivich and Andrew Shatté, *The Resilience Factor: 7 Keys to Finding Your Inner Strength and Overcoming Life's Hurdles* (Harmony, 2003).

27 Sinek, *Start with Why: How Great Leaders Inspire Everyone to Take Action.*

28 Frank Vertosick Jr., *When the Air Hits Your Brain: Tales from Neurosurgery* (W. W. Norton & Company, 2008).

29 Jim Collins, *Good to Great: Why Some Companies Make the Leap . . . And Others Don't* (Harper Business, 2001).

30 Chamine, *Positive Intelligence: Why Only 20% of Teams and Individuals Achieve Their True Potential and How You Can Achieve Yours.*

31 See Vitalsigns-book.com/resources.

32 Albert Mehrabian, *Silent Messages: Implicit Communication of Emotions and Attitudes* (Wadsworth Pub Co, 2nd edition, 1980).

33 Covey, *The 7 Habits of Highly Effective People.*

34 https://www.ccl.org/articles/leading-effectively-articles/5-ways-avoid-derailing-career/

35 Goldsmith, *What Got You Here Won't Get You There: How Successful People Become Even More Successful.*

36 Brown, *Dare to Lead: Brave Work. Tough Conversations. Whole Hearts.*

Dr. James (Jim) Ice is an organizational sociologist, strategic leadership advisor, public speaker, and educator. He is the owner of NorthStar Learning, a strategy development and talent management consulting company located in Pittsburgh, PA. (www.jimice.org).

For over thirty-five years, he has built his reputation as a trusted advisor to thousands of leaders across the globe. Dr. Ice's specialty is coaching physician leaders to build their personal leadership acumen as they address issues of strategy, workforce optimization, and team development in today's dynamic health care environment. Jim earned a master's degree in organizational strategy and a doctorate in leadership and holds several industry certifications, including Board Certified Executive Coach (CCE) and certified Gallup Strengths Coach.